D1632472

C015570642

THE LAST YEARS OF STEAM
— AROUND THE —
MIDLANDS

THE LAST YEARS OF STEAM
— AROUND THE —
MIDLANDS

FROM THE PHOTOGRAPHIC ARCHIVE
OF THE LATE A. J. MAUND

MICHAEL CLEMENS

FONTHILL

Above: Taken at one of Alan's favourite locations just to the north of Fernhill Heath station, as a '73xxx' catches the morning sun in a winter wonderland.

Page 1: 'Jubilee' No. 45682 *Trafalgar* will soon be heading south from Bromsgrove on a lovely October 1963 evening.

Page 2: Alan travelled around the narrow gauge Scaldwell ironstone system in Northamptonshire on 14 August 1963 behind the quarry's eponymous locomotive.

FONTHILL MEDIA
www.fonthillmedia.com

First published 2013

Typeset in 10.5pt on 13pt Sabon LT Std
Typesetting by Fonthill Media
Printed in the UK

ISBN 978-1-78155-129-5

Connect with us

 facebook.com/fonthillmedia twitter.com/fonthillmedia

Introduction

My interest in railways came about because of the enthusiasm of my late father C. N. 'Jim' Clemens. He travelled all over the country filming the fast disappearing railways and the steam locomotives that worked on them, and provided it was not during school time, I would generally be with him. Of course, I got to know most of my father's railway pals over the years, some would come with us on trips, or perhaps visit the family house in Pershore, Worcestershire, to watch the films, whilst others would be met at railway society meetings; one of these pals was A. J. Maund.

Alan James Maund was born on 1 August 1930 at Stourbridge Road, Halesowen. His father was in the Worcestershire Constabulary, and over the years the family moved to various police stations in the county, including Bredon and Malvern. Alan married Wendy Waddoup at Powick church on 11 August 1962 and they were blessed with two children, Sally and Paul. Alan seems to have had a natural artistic ability and pursued this at Malvern Art College, later becoming the chief advertising designer at Clements Brothers of Stoke Prior near Bromsgrove. Alan died on 10 May 1983; he was only fifty-two years of age.

Alan's love of anything with steam will be easily seen throughout this book, with the photographs in it, all taken by Alan, dating from 1957 to 1966. It is largely a vanished world, and the mix of photographs will, I hope, appeal to railway enthusiasts, modellers, and those with an interest in local history. The end of the steam era coincided with the introduction of their diesel replacements, and many enthusiasts at the time had a deliberate policy of ignoring the new interlopers. But not Alan, and they do make appearances in this book, even including a few of the early electric classes. This was also the time that saw the closure of so much of the rural railway network in the area, but luckily, Alan had the foresight to film all of this and the infrastructure that was disappearing with it.

A vivid recollection of mine as a young lad was my late father being extremely upset when he learned from the widow of local railway photographer F. J. Arthur, whose work regularly appeared in *The Railway Magazine* in the 1930s, that she had thrown away all of his photographs not realising their historical value; a lifetime's archive was lost. Luckily, Wendy Maund had the foresight to mention

Alan Maund is sitting on the locomotive at Dr Brian Rogers's 7¼-inch system at Porter's Hill Farm near Fernhill Heath, Worcester.

Alan's photographic collection to a mutual friend and fellow enthusiast, the late Dr. Brian Rogers of Worcester. As a result, Alan's work lives on in the film shows I do around the country, and now in this book.

Alan had a particular passion for narrow gauge industrial steam locomotives, and felt by the late 1950s that they were on the verge of extinction. He became aware of one such locomotive in a derelict condition at R. P. Beard's Hill Farm at Brockamin in Worcestershire (the Beard family ran a delicatessen at the top of Castle Street in Worcester). The year was 1959, and the engine concerned was an 0-4-0 saddle tank of the 'Wren' class, built by Kerr Stuart of Stoke-on-Trent in 1918 with a works number of 3114. Mr Beard agreed immediately to the idea of preservation and rendered every possible assistance, and by 1961, it was in working condition. It ran on Alan's own private railway at his father's house, the so-called Hindlip & District Light Railway; today, the locomotive is on the Bala Lake Railway in Wales. Alan produced a book, although it was never published, detailing his restoration of the locomotive, and Wendy has asked me to put this marvellous record of the work involved on my website – michaelclemensrailways. co.uk. It will also give you an idea of Alan's artistic abilities, as it includes line drawings done by him in addition to photographs. I asked Wendy how he managed to get the excellent quality text printed in 1961, the answer came back that he didn't have it printed and that it was all hand-written.

My first contact with Alan was in the 1960s when he ran the Worcester sub-branch of the Railway Correspondence & Travel Society. However, my late mother (born 1923) remembered him as a boy when her father was a sergeant at Malvern Police Station. Alan's artistic ability has already been mentioned, and he painted a number of historical railway scenes, many of which Wendy still has. It was one of these framed paintings, of MR 2-4-0 No. 1305 hauling a train locally, that was first prize in an RCTS competition organised by Alan at Worcester. I was aged only about seventeen at the time, but managed to beat off the opposition and win the first prize. When I lived with my parents this painting had pride of place on my bedroom wall, and today still hangs in my railway room.

I think it was at Prince Henry's Grammar School, Evesham, where I studied North American geography to both 'O' and 'A' level, that I first became aware of the problems there could be in identifying a particular area. No consensus of opinion existed on how to define the boundaries of the Western Plains of the United States, and exam questions were asked on the subject. Should it be physical features, the western boundary of the Rocky Mountains was fairly obvious. But what about the eastern physical boundary that was far more blurred? Perhaps the 15-inch or 20-inch isohyet (a line on a map joining places of similar rainfall amounts) would form a better boundary? Or should the area be defined pedalogically (soil type), vegetationally, or even agriculturally? Others promoted using lines of longitude, and there are no doubt other parameters that I have forgotten over the years since I was at school. However, from just the above I am sure you can appreciate some of the pitfalls waiting for anybody involved in trying to identify a particular area.

In a photograph that is believed to date from the summer of 1959, restoration of Kerr Stuart No. 3114 has only just begun at Alan's father's house in Hindlip, Worcester.

Having lived in the Midlands all my life, it still comes as a surprise the places that people and organisations include in the area and those that they do not. Watching the different coverage areas of the BBC and ITV Midlands regional TV news here in Worcestershire can be quite an eye-opener, and it still seems rather strange to me when places on the east coast get mentioned; apparently the 2001 census even included Norfolk and Suffolk in the Midlands. However, at the end of the day it seems there is no strict definition of the Midlands, and it does not correspond to any current administrative area. So in choosing the title of *The Last Years of Steam Around The Midlands*, I was looking for some form of wording that would broadly identify with the photographs that Alan had taken.

As Alan lived close to Worcester and there is much film taken in the area, I felt it would be appropriate to follow the various routes out of 'The Faithful City', so-called because Worcester remained loyal to the King in the Civil War, to achieve coverage across the Midlands. It was the Oxford, Worcester & Wolverhampton Railway that was the first to enter the city in 1850, and as Worcester was centrally located on their system, we see the main workshops and depots built by them that were still in use over a century later. The last of the GWR express routes to London (Paddington) that remained totally steam hauled was that from Worcester, and both on the shed and in Shrub Hill Station we have our first view of the 'Castle' class express locomotives, together with other familiar and not so familiar types, plus their diesel replacements. Alan's first use of colour film (Kodachrome) came in 1959, and an example is seen at Stoulton as we head east to reach Honeybourne in

1965 (filmed with Agfa CT18). Here, we see for the first time the typical, very poor external condition, with name plates removed, of the remaining GWR 4-6-0s in their final year. In the late 1950s, much work was done at Honeybourne and on the old Stratford-upon-Avon & Midland Junction Railway for the benefit of iron ore traffic from the East Midlands to South Wales, and we see examples of this. Yet by 1965, ore was being imported, and all the work from a few years earlier was now worthless scrap. At Moreton-in-Marsh are the original terminal buildings, and now demolished for a supermarket, of the tramway from Stratford-upon-Avon that had its origins in a scheme promoted as 'the first railway ever surveyed in the world'. Seven miles further along the OWWR brings us to Kingham, a railway location that has changed dramatically since the early 1960s. I was amazed recently while chatting to younger local residents and newcomers to the area to find they had no knowledge whatsoever of the extensive railway infrastructure that once existed at Kingham, a one-time junction with branches to both Cheltenham and Chipping Norton, together with a flyover that by-passed the station. The majority of Alan's photographs have no date or location on them, and I have spent much time and effort sorting them all out, hopefully correctly. An example for which there can be no doubt over its exact date is that of Sir Winston Churchill's funeral train, passing slowly through Oxford on 30 January 1965, with people standing to attention on the platform. Also at Oxford on the engine shed is the pioneer 'Western' diesel in its desert sand livery.

To travel south by rail from Worcester involves branching off the Oxford line we have just travelled along at Norton Junction. Here, the Cathedrals Express is seen in 1963, complete with name board and hauled by the locomotive specially renamed in 1957 for this service, No. 7005 *Sir Edward Elgar*. Our first stop along the old Birmingham & Gloucester Railway is at Wadborough, bathed in the evening sunshine of 12 October 1963. Here, and not for the first or last time, Alan's wife Wendy makes an appearance; perhaps Alan was following the style of photographer G. F. Heiron whose wife regularly appeared in his railway photographs published in this era. Ashchurch Station was regarded as one of the country's curiosities, and received praise for its Midland Railway architecture, particularly the pillared glass canopy over the platform; it was also the junction for two branches, both of which Alan filmed. Standing in the sunshine in 1959 outside Tewkesbury locomotive shed is one of the country's locomotive curiosities, Stanier 0-4-4T No. 41900, while at Ripple on Saturday 12 August 1961, the last regular passenger service on the branch departs for Upton-on-Severn. The other branch from Ashchurch is first seen in that bad winter of 1962/63, with the snow still on the ground, and we travel along the line to Ashton-under-Hill, Evesham, Harvington, and Broom Junction. In addition to British Railways locomotives, Alan had a special affection for small industrial engines, and at Gloucester Power Station, one of the fireless variety was in use. From Gloucester, we take the 'push-pull' service to Stroud and up the Golden Valley, and at Kemble, we are witness to an experiment by BR into improving the economics of the rural branch lines to Tetbury and Cirencester. Alan visited the famous railway works at Swindon in both 1963 and 1964, the most southerly place included in this book. Amongst a handful of photographs taken here, there is one of Wendy Maund standing in front of the pioneer lightweight 'Warship' D800 *Sir Brain Robertson*, taken on Perutz colour film. A regret of Wendy's is that she has no recollection of this, or many of the other times she was with Alan on his railway expeditions. She wishes she could remember, and would then have been able to answer more of the questions that I have been asking her.

The Worcester & Hereford Railway proved an expensive line to build with viaducts and tunnels, but it was the final link that allowed the monopoly of Brunel's broad gauge to be broken for the transport of coal from South Wales to London by rail. The elevated Worcester (Foregate Street) Station is on a costly section of both substantial embankments and viaducts about a mile in length. At Bransford Road Junction, the delightful branch to Suckley and Bromyard is taken; a scene of rural tranquillity that survived until the summer of 1964. A large railway permanent way depot was established at Newland in the Second World War, with the Malvern Hills behind it, and the ingredients were here for Alan to take a lovely panoramic photograph. At Ledbury was one of the tunnels on the line. Steeply graded and of restricted bore, it was regarded as one of the most foul in the country, and we see a coal train being banked into it from the station in 1963. At Hereford, Collett 0-6-0 No. 2242 starts us on a trip along the line to Ross-on-Wye, including a journey down the freight only branch through Kerne Bridge and Lydbrook Tunnel to the large cable works at Lydbrook Junction behind another Collett 0-6-0. Continuing on our passenger train east from Ross-on-Wye, we spend time in 1964 at the delightful country station of Mitcheldean Road, watching the activity before a visit to the junction at Grange Court. This part of our journey, broadly to the south-west of Worcester, finishes in a remote area of the Forest of Dean on the steeply graded branch to Whitecliff Quarry in December 1965, just before the elimination of steam in the area.

Alan and Wendy Maund lived just north of Worcester, and quite close to Fernhill Heath Station, which is seen in 1959. An important freight contract that had been won by BR was for the transport of oil from the refinery at Fawley, Southampton, to Bromford Bridge, Birmingham, and these trains were routed through Fernhill Heath. Droitwich Spa is witness to a sight much sought after by enthusiasts, one of the large 2-10-0 freight locomotives hauling a passenger train. Another, class leader No. 92000, is seen on more usual duties hauling an empty oil train along the strange section of railway that ran parallel to, but avoided both Droitwich and Worcester, strange in that for about 100 years it was one of the longest sections of track in the country with no intermediate passenger stations. From Stoke Works, and close by Alan's place of work at Stoke Prior, we travel up the section quadrupled by the LMS in the early 1930s before arrival at Bromsgrove, home to the steepest sustained main-line railway incline in Great Britain - the famous Lickey Bank. All through the steam era and beyond, a fleet of banking locomotives were ready every hour of every day to help push heavy trains up the steep gradient. Amongst a handful of photographs here is one of Bromsgrove putting on its grandest sight: four banking locomotives helping push

Alan's own locomotive was in working order by 1961; it is now on the Bala Lake Railway in Wales.

up one of the very heavy oil trains from Fawley to Birmingham. The surprisingly intensly used branch line from Longbridge through Rubery and Hunnington to Halesowen involved passing over the weight-restricted viaduct at Dowery Dell, and as a result, it proved to be one of the last homes of Johnson's lightweight 0-6-0s, which had their origins as far back as 1875.

The last commercial use of steam locomotives in Worcestershire was at Stourport Power Station, and these are seen before a trip along the Severn Valley and its branches, which begins at Bewdley. One of the GWR railcars introduced from 1940, specifically to improve the finances of rural branch line passenger services, is seen at Cleobury Mortimer on the route that terminated at Woofferton Junction, a station that seemed to suffer a confusion of alternative spellings. Today, Bridgnorth is the northern terminus of the preserved Severn Valley Railway, but Alan photographed the station just before the line closed as a through route in 1963, and we see an Ivatt 2-6-2T simmering away in the evening sunshine. A town that didn't really exist in the era of this book was Telford. However, Alan regularly visited the area, filming the railway activity from 1962 to 1966, and included are Coalport (LNWR), Madeley Junction, and Wellington. Wagon enthusiasts will enjoy the sight here of a freight train that includes two special cattle vans (SCVs) for prize cattle and accompanying drover. After Shrewsbury, a trip is made in March 1962 to one of the more obscure lines in Britain, to what was left of the

One of Alan's paintings; the author won this as first prize in a 1968 railway society competition.

Snailbeach District Railways in rural Shropshire that was worked by a Fordson tractor, and the most westerly place seen in this book.

We quickly arrive at our most northerly point, which is Crewe, and the place the Grand Junction Railway chose as the site for their locomotive works. Steam, diesel, and electric locomotives were all at Crewe in the early 1960s, and amongst a handful or so of photographs included from this famous railway town there is one of the LMS diesel shunters that dated from 1939, one of the Crosti 2-10-0s, now converted back to conventional operation and looking very smart after a visit to the works, and one of the experimental 'Black 5s' produced after the Second World War with Caprotti valve gear. More electric action is seen at Rugeley (Trent Valley) not long after energisation of the overhead wires, before we venture up onto Cannock Chase in the snow. At Hednesford, see celebrity industrial locomotive *Cannock Wood*, which had once been owned by the London, Brighton & South Coast Railway. A common sight from the early 1960s was rows and rows of condemned steam locomotives awaiting the cutter's torch. Up until then, the railway's own workshops would often cope with this, but due to both the change from steam power and a contraction of business done by the railways, so many were being condemned that private contractors had to be used. One such contractor was Cashmore's of Great Bridge, and we see a sad GWR 0-4-2T No. 1424 ready to begin its last journey. A class of locomotive with legendary haulage powers were the LNWR 'Super Ds', whose heritage dated back to when Queen Victoria was on the throne. Alan visited Bescot shed in October 1963 to see some of the last few in service. In Birmingham itself, we see both New Street and Snow Hill Stations, before a visit to Tyseley shed, where another celebrity locomotive was present in January 1965. Inside the shed in poor light and looking in poor condition, but still in service, was No. 92220 *Evening Star*, the last steam locomotive constructed by BR. Then, it is along the GWR main line to Banbury via Hatton and on to Hook Norton, calling at Southam Cement Works on the way. The narrow gauge system here was a favourite of Alan's, and as something rather different from the usual, the locomotives here followed a geological theme for their names, with such gems as *Mesozoic, Triassic*, and *Jurassic*.

Heading further east we arrive at Bicester (London Road) in 1963, which as this book is being written, seems likely to soon be enjoying a rapid period of railway expansion, with both the partial restoration of the so-called Varsity Line from Oxford towards Cambridge, and the building of a new spur, allowing Chiltern Railways to run a direct service from Oxford to London through this station. Verney Junction is another station on the Varsity Line, the one-time northern limit of the Metropolitan Railway from London, and here, everything was being watched over by a rather unlikely-looking bird. The very furthest east in this book is Huntingdon, a photograph I was unable to identify. However, thanks are due to the chairman of the Great Northern Railway Society who was able to recognise the location and provide details about it. The ironstone railways of the East Midlands were another of Alan's favourites, and first seen is the metre gauge system (a rare gauge for Britain) to Finedon Quarries near Wellingborough in 1966. Then, it is over to Brixworth on the LNWR line from Northampton to Market Harborough in 1963 where there were two systems, standard gauge at Hanging Houghton and narrow gauge at Scaldwell. A visit is also made to BR at Market Harborough itself, where both steam and diesel are seen, before moving on to a railway town that is no longer on the railway map – Woodford Halse. The photographs finish with scenes at Burton-on-Trent, Derby, in 1957, and Uttoxeter, before concluding at Fernhill Heath.

As was mentioned earlier in this introduction, a challenge for me has been identifying Alan's photographs, the majority of which have no date or location with them. I would like here to specifically thank various societies and individuals, in no particular order, who have been kind enough to freely give me their help: the Sutton Coldfield Railway Society, the Monmouthshire Railway Society, the Severn Valley Railway Museum, the Severn Valley Railway Association (Stourbridge Branch), the Shirley Railway Club, Mark Ratcliffe (Burton Railway Society), George Howe (Great Northern Railway Society), Wayne Finch (Gloucestershire Warwickshire Railway), Alan Brain (Chipping Norton Railway Club), and Mike Morris (Gloucester Film Makers). The Cheltenham Railway Action Photographers (or CRAP as they refer to themselves) deserve an extended thanks, their depth of knowledge, both railway and photographic, is astonishing, and includes dates, locations, and details, plus a seemingly instant recall of locomotive allocations from fifty or more years ago. Between them all, an encyclopedic archive is held in their minds and their help was enthusiastically and unreservedly given; the antithesis of their CRAP acronym.

To conclude, Wendy Maund has said how indebted she is to me for the time, patience, and effort I have put in to create this lasting record of her late husband's work. Nonetheless, I think we are all indebted to Wendy for having the good judgement to save Alan's photographs for posterity and to allow the archive to be enjoyed by all.

Michael Clemens
Pershore, Worcestershire
October 2012

Below: Victorian-built Johnson '2F' No. 58138 is almost lost in the undergrowth as it works a freight train between Halesowen and Rubery.

The Photographic Archive of the Late A. J. Maund

The first railway to serve the city of Worcester was opened by the Oxford, Worcester & Wolverhampton Railway in 1850. Being situated about midway along the OWWR, Worcester was a logical place to build major servicing facilities, and much of the infrastructure is still visible in this summer 1964 panorama taken from Railway Walk. The engine shed complex consisted of two separate buildings: to the right is the four-road goods engine depot, while just left of centre is the three-road passenger engine depot; the large buildings further to the left formed the main OWWR workshops. Fifty-two acres of land were purchased in 1852 for this to the west of Shrub Hill station, which is just visible above the roof of the passenger depot. All this finished with the end of steam at Worcester at the end of 1965. On 31 December, the author's friend Eric Parker visited for one last time, and at the workshops, was given the surviving notebooks plus returns sheets for the period from 1956 to 1965.

Looking very smart, but with a rather non-standard smoke-box number plate, No. 7022 *Hereford Castle* stands at Worcester shed (85A) in the summer of 1964, with the substantial buildings of the OWWR works behind it. Due to the unreliability of the diesels that had taken over the Worcester to Paddington services in September 1963, steam had enjoyed an Indian summer on the route, and No. 7022 is probably the standby locomotive. However, this was now coming to an end, and the last steam substitution the author saw was on 14 July 1964, and this with No. 7022. *Hereford Castle* led something of a charmed life, as it survived being allocated to Plymouth Laira shed long after most services had gone over to diesels, being used on the depot's only regular steam turn in the summer of 1963 – the daily Plymouth to Goodrington (Paignton) excursion. No. 7022 was transferred to Hereford in November 1963 and reached Worcester in April 1964. reallocation to Gloucester came in the October, followed by withdrawal in June 1965.

It is 19 April 1965, and Worcester shed is host to a rare visitor, modified 'Battle of Britain' class No. 34089 *602 Squadron*. This date was Easter Monday in 1965, and a very grimy No. 34089 has come to Worcester for servicing after working an excursion train from the Southern Region – *602 Squadron*'s usual sphere of operation at this time was between Waterloo, Bournemouth, and Weymouth. The best steam coal in the world is said to be that from South Wales, and this was the GWR's preferred choice at most of their depots. Although Welsh steam coal burns well in the confined space of a locomotive's firebox, a problem is that it is friable, which means that it easily crumbles to dust and so has to be handled with care. As a result, the GWR used manual instead of mechanical handling of coal. An exception was here at Worcester (and also Southall), where the coaling hoist system being used to refuel No. 34089 was installed in 1944.

The GWR's first diesel mechanical railcar No. 1 was put into service on 4 December 1933 in the Reading area on local services. No. 18 was built in 1937 and incorporated some new features, such as being able to haul a tail load of 60 tons and being fitted with standard drawgear. A further batch of twenty was authorised in February 1938 and based on No. 18, of which fifteen, including No. 20 seen here, were for branch and subsidiary services. All entered service between June 1940 and February 1942. In June 1947, Worcester had seven allocated, the highest of any depot, and they saw much use on the Severn Valley line. The last survivors were mostly in the Worcester area, but all had been withdrawn by October 1962. W20W, its BR number, remained in a derelict condition in the yards by Worcester shed for quite some time, as seen here, but was preserved by the Kent & East Sussex Railway where it still is today.

In May 1964 two of the '16xx' class lightweight pannier tanks, Nos 1639 & 1661, were allocated to Worcester specifically for working the 'Vinegar Branch', the only steam locomotives allowed on this line. The Worcester Railways Act of 1870 authorised vinegar manufacturers Hill, Evans & Co (at their own expense) to extend an already existing siding onwards to the vinegar works in Lowesmoor; the branch was only about half a mile long in total. The summer 1962 Gloucester District Freight Working Timetable shows that Worcester shunting engine duty No. F.01 consisted only of a Monday morning vinegar trip and a Monday to Friday afternoon trip, followed by general shunting duties away from the vinegar branch, a total of forty-two hours duty per week. The problem for Nos 1639 & 1661 was that the last train on the branch ran on 5 June 1964, and hauled by No. 1639, with formal closure about a month later. The photograph of a very decrepit looking No. 1639 at the rear of the goods engine shed at Worcester dates from the following winter, the locomotive having been withdrawn in November 1964. It was cut up at Steel Supply Co. (Western) Ltd near Swansea. That of No. 1661 dates from March 1964 when the locomotive was the Worcester shed pilot. Particularly noticeable is the spark-arresting chimney, designed for use in places such as ordinance factories, where hot embers of coal are an obvious problem. No. 1661 had been built at Swindon as late as 1955, but was withdrawn in July 1964 and succumbed to the cutter's torch at Birds Ltd.

Photographed from inside Worcester's passenger shed on a 1964 summer's day are No. 7252 and an unidentified pannier tank. No. 7252 is a member of the only class of 2-8-2 tank engine to run on British Railways, although it had begun its life as a 2-8-0T. GWR chief mechanical engineer G. J. Churchward introduced the '42xx' class 2-8-0Ts in 1910 for heavy mineral traffic in South Wales, and they proved a success. However, the 1920s saw a considerable drop in coal exports, and many later members of the class were placed in storage as their coal and water capacity, while ideal for short journeys in the Welsh valleys, precluded them from a wider use. Churhward's successor C. J. Collett modified the 2-8-0Ts to increase both water and coal capacities by adding a bolt-on extension at the rear, including a trailing wheel. Eventually, there were fifty-four of these 2-8-2Ts. No. 7252 appears coaled up and ready, possibly to work back to South Wales on the 9.45 p.m. freight to Pontypool Road.

Taken from the down platform at Worcester (Shrub Hill) we find 'Hymek' class D7090 running light engine. A clue to what is happening is the four-character train identification – 1A85. The Working Timetable operative from 9 September 1963 lists 1A85 as the 2.05 p.m. Hereford to Paddington express with a 10 minute stop here from 3.00 p.m., presumably to change locomotives, with the stock of the London train behind the 'Hymek'. D7090 looks to be in tip-top external condition, perhaps even pristine, as its date of entry to traffic is listed as 24 September 1963. The two middle roads seen here survived until June 1973, and they also used to have scissors-crossings connecting with both the up and down platform lines to help with the splitting and re-forming of trains. Many early diesels suffered the same fate as latter-day steam locomotives with quite short lives, and D7090 was a typical example, being withdrawn in June 1972 after a life of less than nine years.

It is August 1963, and regular steam haulage of the Paddington expresses is fast coming to a close, as No. 7025 *Sudeley Castle* pulls away from Worcester (Shrub Hill) for another 120½-mile run up to London. The smaller than usual signals on the left are used where space is limited; the arms are modified so that they pivot near their centre. *Sudeley Castle* had been one of the very last class members to receive attention in the main ex-GWR workshops at Swindon, receiving a light intermediate repair in December 1962. In May 1964, a special final high-speed run from London to Plymouth and return was organised, hauled by 'Castles' in both directions on record-breaking schedules. As regular daily express work for the class had ceased, surviving locomotives were specially tested on the Worcester route to check their suitability. No. 7025 was selected to be the reserve locomotive at Taunton and took over the down special following a failure en route with the now preserved No. 4079 *Pendennis Castle*.

Standing in the fading light, with its lit oil headcode lamps prominent, in the bay platform at Worcester (Shrub Hill), and adjacent to that, from which No. 7025 has just departed in the previous picture, is the now preserved No. 7029 *Clun Castle*. This locomotive was preserved directly out of BR service at the end of 1965 by Mr Pat Whitehouse, having achieved fame following its performance on the 9 May 1964 Plymouth high-speed special mentioned previously, where it set the record time for steam between Plymouth and Bristol. It was the very last 'Castle' in BR service and was much sought after on enthusiast's specials, which is why it is waiting here. Z40 is reporting code for the Locomotive Club of Great Britain's 'Western Venturer' rail-tour that ran on 6 February 1965. No. 7029 had hauled this from Paddington to Gloucester via Bristol, and after running light engine to Worcester, will haul it back to London with a scheduled departure time from here of 4.24 p.m.

Photographed in January 1960 from the Perry Wood Walk railway bridge, the up 'Cathedrals Express' has just left Worcester Shrub Hill station on its journey to London Paddington. There is plenty of business being done at the Metal Box Co. Ltd on the right; they had opened this works in 1931 and it still has a rail connection today. For the centenary of the birth of composer Edward Elgar in 1957, the premier express along this route was named the 'Cathedrals Express', and locomotive No. 7005 was renamed *Sir Edward Elgar* in his honour. Hauling the 'Cathedrals Express' today is another celebrity, the last express locomotive made by the GWR at Swindon before nationalisation, No. 7007 *Great Western*, although it was actually built in 1946 as *Ogmore Castle* and renamed in January 1948. Close inspection will reveal that No. 7007 has a single chimney. It was out-shopped from Swindon in April 1961 with both a double chimney and four-row superheater, but that didn't stop withdrawal in February 1963.

Right: As a seated Wendy Maund enjoys some evening sunshine in June 1963, the down 'Cathedrals Express', complete with headboard, hurries through Stoulton to maintain its 7.55 p.m. arrival time at Worcester (Shrub Hill), having left Paddington at 5.15 p.m. The timings for this train are based on a 'Castle' hauling a maximum tare load of 300 tons, which corresponds to about nine coaches. Worcester allocated 'Modified Hall' No. 6992 *Arborfield Hall* looks to be hauling ten, plus No. 6992 is only rated at class 5, as opposed to class 7 for a 'Castle'. The author, at this time, was a pupil at Prince Henry's Grammar School, Evesham, from where excellent views of the Paddington expresses could be had. Although Worcester shed had a full complement of 'Castles', they clearly had complete confidence in their 'Modified Halls', which would be seen turn and turn about on the London services. Stoulton signal box was normally switched out by 1963, only opening for traffic purposes, and it closed completely on 19 April 1964.

Above: This is Stoulton Station, between Worcester and Evesham, with a 'Modified Hall' passing through on a down express, and although undated, the photograph is believed to have been taken in September 1959. The railway here was built by the OWWR, and on 1 May 1852, a special train ran from Stourbridge to Evesham with normal service starting two days later. By July 1852, double track was in use between Norton Junction and Evesham. This is a quite remote location with only a few houses locally, the village of Stoulton being some distance away. Originally, there was no station here at all and it was not opened until 20 February 1899, nearly forty-seven years after the line had opened. Despite this, the fairly substantial station building and platforms are clean and tidy, plus the garden looks well cared for. However, everything came to an end from 3 January 1966, when Stoulton and many of the other rural stations along this route were closed.

There is plenty of railway infrastructure to see in this lovely photograph taken at Honeybourne, looking east with the Cotswolds in the background from the bridge on the Bidford-on-Avon road – the one-time Roman Icknield (or Ryknild) Street. The date is 3 July 1965 and 'Hall' class No. 6921 *Borwick Hall* is threading a freight over the point-work towards Worcester. The locomotive is in the typical condition of GWR 4-6-0s in 1965, the last full year any remained in service. It has no smoke-box number plate, no name plate, and appears not to have a cab-side number plate or shed plate either; you wonder how Alan was able to identify it! Most of these plates were taken off from the beginning of 1965, as the authorities were well aware of their value to enthusiasts, and there had already been cases of theft. In the middle distance is Honeybourne Station south signal box. When the Oxford to Worcester line was singled in 1971, this was converted to a ground frame.

A poor quality photograph, but of great significance for the Cheltenham to Stratford-upon-Avon line. By the summer of 1965, there was very little in the way of steam-hauled passenger trains in Worcestershire, an exception being the Saturdays only holidaymaker services from the West Midlands to the resorts of the south-west, and these were steam hauled to and from Bristol. It has already been explained how No. 7029 *Clun Castle* became something of a celebrity locomotive, and it was specially requested to work the very final northbound working of these services. No. 7029 is seen passing Honeybourne West Loop signal box in very poor light on 4 September 1965, hauling the 12.20 p.m. Penzance to Wolverhampton (Low Level) that it had taken over at Bristol. This new signal box and associated sidings, plus other connected works at Stratford-upon-Avon and Fenny Compton – all to do with re-routing of ironstone traffic – fully opened in 1960, but five years later were all surplus to requirements.

People usually think that GWR means Great Western Railway. However, in Victorian times it was referred to by some as the Great Way Round. This was because it served a number of important places by indirect routes, such as London to South Wales via Gloucester, and much effort was spent building new direct lines, such as the Severn Tunnel. Another problem route for the GWR was that from Gloucester to Birmingham, In the Victorian era, the service was via Newent, Ledbury, Worcester, and Stourbridge Junction. In the early years of the twentieth century a direct route was opened via Cheltenham, Toddington, Honeybourne, Stratford-upon-Avon, and Henley-in-Arden, using both newly built and existing lines. In a photograph taken on 3 July 1965, the afternoon service from Leamington Spa General to Gloucester Central is about to pass under the Stanton Road bridge near Toddington. Today, the Gloucestershire Warwickshire Railway is restoring this line to working order, and thanks go to their Wayne Finch for help with identification of this photograph.

On 14 September 1963, Alan travelled on the Railway Enthusiasts' Club 'Chiltern 200' rail tour, and it is seen taking water behind GWR 2-6-2T No. 6111 at what was left of the Stratford-upon-Avon & Midland Junction Railway Station at Stratford. Passenger services ceased in 1952, but there was considerable freight traffic for some years after, mainly ironstone from the East Midlands to South Wales. Up to 1960, these trains carried on straight behind the special via the 1942 built spur at Broom, Evesham, and Ashchurch, before heading on to South Wales. It was realised that the section to Broom from Stratford, about 7¾ miles long, could be closed, and the traffic routed on the GWR Stratford to Cheltenham line if a connecting link was constructed between the SMJR and GWR lines. A double-track connection approximately 22 chains long was built, and can be seen curving to the left behind the train. It was first worked on 12 June 1960, but saw its last train in 1965.

The same tour is now seen further along the SMJR at Kineton, and a stop was scheduled here from 3.12 to 3.22 p.m. The trip had begun from the old LNWR Rewley Road Station in Oxford at 10.15 a.m. In conjunction with the other works already mentioned at Stratford and Honeybourne, a new connection was added at Fenny Compton that allowed South Wales-bound ironstone trains from Banbury to travel through Kineton, and the loop here was extended from 16 to 27 chains. The last passenger train had called on 5 April 1952, and by this time, the platforms had been cut back. There are some freight wagons in the goods yard, but this too came to an end on 11 November 1963. The signal box, partly visible over the first coach, was not closed until 22 August 1966 despite the last through train running on 24 April 1965 (a Stephenson Locomotive Society special); the idea was to prevent vandalism with signalmen still attending their boxes to test the instruments.

Right, above and below: These photographs are both taken at Moreton-in-Marsh, and the first is looking west from the A44 road bridge. The entire main line of the OWWR was laid with mixed gauge (for broad and standard gauge trains) from Oxford to Wolverhampton, and evidence of the wider gauge can still be seen at Moreton-in-Marsh Station, where the gap between the up and down tracks is wider than normal. R. A. Cooke's series of 'Track Layout Diagrams' have proved very useful in dating these photographs. The crossover between the up and down tracks in the foreground originally extended to the siding where the goods shed is, but it was taken out of use in December 1961 and there is no trace of it in the photograph. The track on the right forms the connection to the by then closed Shipston-on-Stour branch, and it is possible to make out the still-existing point work to two sidings that have been taken up. These are both listed as removed in April 1964, so these photographs date from no earlier than the summer of 1964. The second photograph shows the station buildings for the very first 'railway' in this part of the Midlands, the Stratford & Moreton Tramway. In fact, the first scheme for this, dated 1820, claimed that it was 'the first railway ever surveyed in the world'. It opened in 1826 for horse-drawn traffic connecting to the canal basin at Stratford-upon-Avon, and although the section from Moreton to Shipston-on-Stour was converted into a 'proper' railway in the 1880s, that onwards to Stratford was last used around 1904.

The REC tour of 14 September 1963 has arrived back at Kingham after a trip to Chipping Norton. Both this branch, and that to Cheltenham, as far as Bourton-on-the-Water, had remained open for freight traffic only after 1962, until complete closure from 7 September 1964. 'Large Prairie' No. 6111, after running round its train between 1.00 p.m. and 1.40 p.m., will then take the tour to Stratford-upon-Avon, as seen earlier in this book, via the south-east curve at Honeybourne that had opened in 1907; interestingly, there are proposals at present to introduce a service from Oxford to Stratford largely following the route to be taken by No. 6111. In front of the rail tour and behind the lovely display of flowers is a diesel multiple unit (DMU) led by car W51104, possibly waiting to form the 1.30 p.m. Saturdays only service to Reading; the tracks that both trains are on were taken out of use from 24 July 1966.

Left, above and below: It is March 1962, and the black & white view is looking west at Kingham. There was no station here when the OWWR opened their main line in 1853; that had to wait until 10 August 1855, when the standard gauge branch to Chipping Norton, seen curving away to the right, was opened. Despite the village of Kingham being close-by, the station was opened as Chipping Norton Junction, changing to Kingham in 1909. The brick built and slate roofed engine shed to the left of the water tank opened in 1913 and originally had a turntable outside the shed entrance. Moving further to the left is Kingham Station signal box, the colour photograph of which is believed to have been taken on 23 July 1966. To the side of the signal box, and spanning the main line to Moreton-in-Marsh, is a double-track steel girder bridge. Opening on 8 January 1906, initially for freight, this bridge allowed through running trains from Banbury and Chipping Norton destined for Cheltenham to avoid reversal at Kingham. The 'Ports to Ports' express ran across it on its journey from Newcastle to South Wales. Coming in on the left is a train from Cheltenham via Bourton-on-the-Water and Stow-on-the-Wold, hauled by No. 5182. From Cheltenham to London it was often quicker, and certainly much shorter, to take the branch train to Kingham and then catch a Worcester to Paddington service, rather than taking a through train via Gloucester, Stroud, and Swindon. Passenger services on both of the branches ceased later in 1962.

Photographed on the same March 1962 day as that at Kingham, No. 5182 is now at Chipping Norton. Previous to 4 June 1951, passenger services carried on northwards to Hook Norton and Banbury. In that year however, there was a national coal shortage, and to conserve supplies, train frequencies were reduced on many lines, plus some of the more lightly used, as here, lost their service. The only section remaining open to passenger traffic was between Chipping Norton and Kingham. It would be something of an understatement to say that this remaining passenger service was sparse, for there were only two trains each way per day to and from Kingham in 1962. This is the sole afternoon train, and No. 5182 has worked the service seen previously in this book from Cheltenham (St. James) to Kingham. This trip to Chipping Norton and back then followed, before heading home to Cheltenham. This could not last, and the end of the passenger service came from 3 December 1962.

No. 5152 pulls out of Chipping Norton on what is believed to be 14 September 1963, with the branch freight train in the period following withdrawal of the passenger service. Unlike Chipping Norton, the single intermediate halt on the branch at Sarsden lost both its freight and passenger service at the same time, 3 December 1962, so No. 5152 will not be doing any business on its way back to Kingham. Before withdrawal of the passenger service, the morning train in both directions on the branch was a mixed train, with second class accommodation only. A mixed train was a familiar feature in the early days of railways, when it was common to see conveyance of both freight and passengers by the same service. However, it became much less common following stringent controls introduced by the 1889 Regulation of Railways Act, in particular, provision of continuous brakes, although it was still permissible. Freight traffic eventually finished and the branch closed completely from 7 September 1964.

Oxford shed, included because it shows the pioneer 'Western' class diesel D1000 *Western Enterprise* in its desert sand livery, Although undated, research has been able to throw some light on an approximate date. The locomotive closest to Alan appears to be No. 7035 *Ogmore Castle*, with the double-chimney that it had received in 1960. Perhaps more importantly, it was an Oxford-allocated engine from November 1962 to March 1963, before it was transferred to Old Oak Common, London, from where it was withdrawn at the beginning of June 1964. The four-character train identification code carried by D1000 is 1A68, which in the summer of 1963 was used for the 12.05 p.m. Hereford to Paddington, departing Oxford at 2.39 p.m. D1000 had entered service in December 1961, and apparently received the small yellow warning panel it is carrying here in November 1962, eventually getting maroon livery in October 1964. *Western Enterprise* was one of the earlier class withdrawals in February 1974. However, seven did survive into preservation.

No. 5014 *Goodrich Castle* arrives at Oxford displaying the lamp code for what appears to be a quite lengthy parcels train, while the crew of BR Standard Class 4 No. 75008 look on stopped at the signals. No. 5014 was a regular performer on the Worcester expresses at the end of steam haulage, having had a heavy intermediate overhaul at Swindon in December 1961. It had been London-allocated since the Second World War, with its 81A shed code prominent. No. 75008 was Oxford-allocated from 1958 to 1964, and is sporting the double-chimney it received in February 1961. Oxford became famous after the Grouping of 1923 as a place where main line passenger engines from all four companies could be seen. The station here dated from 1852 and was beginning to look rather decrepit by the early 1960s. The long-desired rebuilding finally came about in 1971, but today, the four running lines are barely adequate for the increasing traffic, and more rebuilding is again on the cards.

Although this Oxford photograph is again undated, there is absolutely no doubt over the exact date, as it is Sir Winston Churchill's funeral train on 30 January 1965. The funeral train ran from Waterloo to Handborough for burial at Blaydon near Blenheim Palace. There could only be one choice for the locomotive, No. 34051 *Winston Churchill*, and it ran with the special Southern Region disc headcode seen here of a 'V for Victory'. It had been planned to run the train through Oxford at line speed, but the train crew were advised that the city's bells would ring muffled peals as they passed through, so they slowed to 20 mph. In fact at stations all along the route, hundreds of people had purchased platform tickets, simply to stand with heads bowed as the train passed. In contrast to Oxford, where as previously mentioned, the poor condition of the station, especially the canopy on the far platform, was clear to see, at Handborough, the peeling paintwork was cleverly disguised with purple drapes.

After our journey east from Worcester we will now head south, as BR Standard Class 5 No. 73093 arrives at Worcester (Shrub Hill) from the north. The service concerned, in this undated photograph, is probably one of the stopping trains between Birmingham (New Street) and Gloucester (Eastgate), which remained largely steam-hauled until closure of many of the rural stations and withdrawal of the service; the last trains running on Saturday 2 January 1965. No. 73093 was allocated to Gloucester from 1961 to 1965, as were other members of this class, and they were regular performers on this service. This locomotive was notable as being one of the few of the class that had had a heavy intermediate repair at Wolverhampton Works, in No. 73093's case during the spring of 1960. Of the four class members allocated to Gloucester at the end of 1964, only No. 73093 survived beyond 1965, and it ended up on the Southern Region to see out the end of steam there in July 1967.

At Norton Junction the route east from Worcester splits: to the left for Evesham and Oxford, to the right, south for Cheltenham and Gloucester. It is June 1963, and No. 7005 *Sir Edward Elgar* has about 3 miles left before bringing the 'Cathedrals Express' into Worcester (Shrub Hill). Surprisingly, considering the OWWR main line is that to the left, the first to be opened was that to the right in 1850, to enable connection with the Birmingham & Gloucester Railway at what is now Abbots Wood Junction (spelt Abbotts Wood in the working timetables the author has). The B&GR had avoided Worcester, and this link formed the first line into the city, the route to Evesham opening in 1852. In 1963, the speed limit in the Oxford direction was 75 mph, and that to Abbots Wood 15 mph. Today, despite some recent re-doubling of the Cotswold Line to Oxford, the route is single track towards Evesham and has been since 1971, but still double to Abbots Wood.

It is 12 October 1963, and Alan plus his wife Wendy, just visible on the station seat, have come to Wadborough to photograph the Locomotive Club of Great Britain's 'Thames, Avon, and Severn' rail tour. It was due to pass at about 4.46 p.m., but was around 50 minutes late, running non-stop from Camp Hill through Birmingham (New Street) to Cheltenham Lansdown behind No. 45552. Coming north is the 4.48 p.m. Gloucester (Eastgate) to Birmingham (New Street) stopping service, due to make its Wadborough call at 5.32 p.m. behind Saltley-allocated 'Black 5' No. 45268, with the sun having nearly set. Interestingly, although not advertised in the public timetable, this local service, plus a number of others in both directions, made calls at Norton Halt (Norton Junction previous to 1959) according to the working timetable. Wadborough station had opened on 15 November 1841 and closed from 4 January 1965. Although there was no signal box here, there was, and still is, a road crossing, plus a B&GR crossing keeper's cottage.

Heading north on 25 February 1961 is Stanier 8F No. 48167, hauling an express freight without continuous brake. The photograph is taken from the A440 road bridge at Defford; a single carriageway at this time, but now a dual carriageway. No. 48167 was one of a wartime batch of fifty of this class built at Crewe between 1941 and 1943, and it has just crossed over the River Avon. To the right in the middle distance are the remains of a water tower, while to the left, largely hidden in the smoke and steam, is Bredon Hill. The signal post in the foreground with strong guying was controlled by Defford signal box, which in 1959 was open from 6.40 a.m. to 9.10 p.m. Monday to Saturday, but switched out at other times. The next signal box to the south at Eckington, open continuously as it controlled a level crossing, was only 1 mile and 8 chains distant, so it was hardly surprising that Defford box closed at the beginning of May 1964.

A Stanier 8F is trundling a southbound freight through Ashchurch in about 1960. The line curving to the right is the branch to Evesham, Alcester, Redditch, and Barnt Green, which paralleled the main line through Bromsgrove, but avoided the notorious Lickey Bank. Ashchurch was also the junction for the Tewkesbury branch to the left, but is not visible in this photograph. The February 1957 *Trains Illustrated* refers to Ashchurch Station as one of the country's curiosities. It praises its Midland Railway architecture, particularly the pillared glass canopy over the platform, and it makes special reference to the refreshment room. The sign for this is just visible in the background by the footbridge, and by 1957, it was not operated by British Transport Catering Services. The article stated that no other refreshment room in Britain had a dart board. But two months later, a letter to the editor pointed out that Ashchurch was not unique, and that the refreshment room at Talyllyn Junction (near Brecon) also had a dart board!

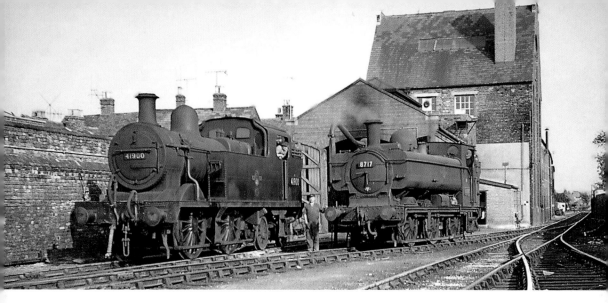

A superb photograph, and taken at Tewkesbury engine shed on 3 October 1959. The shed was on the original line to the town's station that had opened in 1840, but which closed in 1864 when the new station on the Upton extension opened. In the late 1950s, the shed normally played host to the Tewkesbury branch locomotive, an Evesham line engine overnight, plus a third that visited for servicing in the day off the Evesham route. On this day, in addition to GWR pannier tank No. 8717 and one of a class of 863, 0-4-4T No. 41900 is present from a rather strange class that totalled just ten. Strange in that the design was Victorian, with the last being built in 1900, although then ten more followed between 1932 and 1933, including No. 41900. By 1958, many of these ten were already out of use, and No. 41900 became the last in service, latterly stored at Wellington (Salop) and taken to Crewe for scrapping on 15 March 1962.

Although undated, by comparing it with that of No. 8717 at Tewkesbury, this photograph at Upton-on-Severn is almost certainly taken on 3 October 1959. Until 1 December 1952, trains carried on to Great Malvern, and it was only the voluble protests of local residents that limited the cuts to just this section, as it had been planned to abandon the service totally. However, the services did not escape without pruning, and at this time, there was only a single train on weekdays from Ashchurch to Upton and two back, plus one extra trip each way on Saturdays. A notable feature at Upton was the embankments. The River Severn is very prone to flooding, and Upton has been isolated many times with the railway forming the only means of communication out of the town. This point was brought up when the closure proposals were published, but it was stated that it would not make economic sense to keep the line open just for times of flood.

The end for passenger services on the Upton-on-Severn branch came on Saturday 12 August 1961, and these photographs are of the last ever Upton bound train from Ashchurch and Tewkesbury at Ripple. The line here had been built as double track, and the Midland Railway doubled the section from Ashchurch to Tewkesbury at the same time. Sadly, the expected revenues never appeared, and the two tracks were hardly justified, as there were a maximum of five passenger trains and two goods each way. Just before the First World War, the up line from Tewkesbury was taken out of use and used for wagon storage. In 1910, the signal box at Ripple was closed and the ground frame, visible in both photographs, added instead; as the connection from this time at Ripple to the sidings was from the down side, it was this fact that determined the up line was taken out of use. By 12 August 1961, the second track had gone, although to the east of Ripple in 1959 a new track alignment and bridge were put in to cross the M50 Motorway. In the last few years of the passenger service, GWR pannier tanks became a common sight, but fittingly at the very end, the MR 0-6-0 No. 43754 from Gloucester (Barnwood) shed was used. The service was normally just one coach, but for this final train two were used, packed with enthusiasts and local residents making their last journey along the line. Freight carried on until 1 June 1963 at both Ripple and Upton, and at Tewkesbury it survived until 2 November 1964.

Taken from an Ashchurch bound service in about 1960, this is the up platform at the old Midland Railway station in Evesham. The station nameboard looks to be a BR replacement of the original, and despite this line's history being associated with the MR and LMS, this nameboard plus the other signage visible on the station is in the brown of the Western Region of BR, under whose jurisdiction the line now came all the way to Barnt Green. There was only passenger accommodation on this side of the station, the footbridge between the two being added about 1905. By the time of this photograph, the ticket office and bookstall had been closed, and intending passengers had to purchase these at the adjacent former GWR station across the station yard. The same combining of facilities at Evesham led to these platforms being numbered 1 and 2, with 3 and 4 being the GWR platforms. Very little of the MR side of Evesham survives today, an exception being this station building.

Left, above and below: Remnants from the severe winter of 1962/63 are visible in these March 1963 monochrome prints, taken at Ashchurch above and Ashton-under-Hill below. The railway from Ashchurch to Evesham, Alcester, Redditch, and Barnt Green was closed as a through route with effect from 1 October 1962, the reason being the condition of the track between Alcester and Evesham. The double-track section from Evesham to Ashchurch stayed open for both freight and passenger traffic, with generally, as here, a Gloucester (Horton Road) based pannier tank plus a single coach, or perhaps two, shuttling back and forth over the 10 miles and 68 chains. As can be seen at Ashchurch, with No. 3745 waiting for custom before departing to Evesham, despite the double track, there was only the single passenger platform for trains on the branch (and also the same here for the Upton branch). As No. 3745 prepares to leave Ashton-under-Hill for Ashchurch in the cold, with the 400kV transmission lines from Hams Hall to Melksham in the background, few would have thought in 1963 that since closure, a private swimming pool has been constructed between the two platforms by the owner of the station buildings. In the spring of 1957, a connection was laid between this route and the GWR line at Evesham, and by the early 1960s, it had made this section on to Ashchurch reasonably busy with through freight trains, very often between Yarnton (Oxford) and South Wales. The passenger service came to an end from 17 June 1963, and the route was totally closed from 9 September 1963.

The Act for the Evesham & Redditch Railway was granted in 1863, and it opened between Evesham and Alcester for freight on 16 June 1866, and passenger traffic on 17 September 1866, with the final section between Alcester and Redditch opening for all traffic on 4 May 1868. Harvington was the first station north of Evesham, and is thought to be seen during 1961 as a southbound service from Redditch draws to a stop, hauled by No. 43013. Beyond the substantial stationmaster's house were the booking office, waiting room, and toilets. Although the station itself had just a single track, there was a signal box at Harvington, just visible on the extreme right behind undergrowth. During 1944, this box was open continuously, but at this time, it was only open on weekdays from 5.45 a.m. until the last service in the evening. The passenger trains calling at Harvington remained largely steam hauled until closure in 1962, with the exception of the summer Sunday service worked by DMUs in the last years.

The colour photograph is of 2-6-4T No. 42137 at Broom Junction in 1960 ready to head south towards Evesham, as indicated by the signals on the right of the gantry. The other signals on the gantry are for the line seen diverging left beyond the bridge to Stratford-upon-Avon, this eventually ended up as a 52 miles long east-west route that connected with the Midland Railway at both ends. The connection at the far end, Ravenstone Wood Junction, allowed direct running to London via Olney and Bedford, while the connection here at Broom (after reversal prior to 1942) gave a direct route to Bristol. The end result of this was that the MR ran express freight trains from Bristol to London via Broom Junction, including banana traffic, and this carried on after the Grouping and formation of the LMS in 1923. The signal partly visible on the right was a starting signal for Stratford trains out of the up platform. The signal box beyond the bridge was known at this time as Broom North, and the author has the register for it from 27 February 1962 until closure on 1 October 1962. The black & white photograph shows the site of Bidford-on-Avon station, just over a mile towards Stratford from Broom Junction and, judging by the rust on the track, taken after complete closure of the line in June 1960. Bidford lost its passenger service in June 1947, and its goods yard on the other side of the bridge shut in March 1960. The booking office was located in the arch of the bridge.

This rather strange looking engine is a fireless locomotive, and it worked at Gloucester Power Station (Castle Meads) until 1969; the prominent church in the background being St Nicholas's in Westgate Street. With no fire inside them, they were very useful in places like paper mills or oil refineries. Another advantage, used here, was that they could run on steam produced by the power station boilers. This fireless locomotive was built by Andrew Barclay of Kilmarnock in 1942, works No. 2126. What appears to be the boiler is actually a well-insulated steam reservoir, initially partly filled with hot water and then charged with high-pressure steam from a stationary boiler. Fully charged, the locomotive could work for a few hours, with recharging taking about 20 minutes, the exhaust from the chimney at the rear being just water vapour. Following closure of the power station, the locomotive was donated to the Dowty Railway Preservation Society at Ashchurch, but is now at the Gloucester Waterways Museum.

Between August 1932 and April 1936, the GWR built seventy-five of these 0-4-2 tank engines. Developed from the '517' class of 1868, they were in fact little more than an updated version of the Victorian class, and this did cause some comment at the time. They were fitted out for 'auto-train' or 'push-pull' operation. In this, they were generally coupled to one or two coaches, the end one of which had a driver's compartment in it, which was mechanically connected to the locomotive. Thus, they could be driven from either end of the train, although the fireman always stayed in the locomotive, and the engine didn't need to run round its coaches at the end of a journey before returning, and so saved time. No. 1453 is taking water at Gloucester Central before heading for Stroud and up the Golden Valley to Chalford. It was allocated to Gloucester from July 1962 until both the service ceased and No. 1453 was withdrawn at the beginning of November 1964.

Above: The '45xx' class of 2-6-2Ts, with 4-feet-7½-inch-diameter wheels, were introduced by GWR chief mechanical engineer G. J. Churchward in 1906. A prototype with smaller wheels had been built in 1904, and designed to work hilly branch lines in Wales and the West Country. Here, it proved a success, but it was felt the original 4-feet-1½-inch wheels rather limited its use. Eventually, there were 175 in the class, with the first 75 having a water capacity of 1,000 gallons, the final 100 having visibly larger tanks capable of holding 1,300 gallons. No. 4564, of the 1,000-gallon variety, is simmering away at the west end of Gloucester Central. They revolutionised services in the West Country, but many were withdrawn from the early 1950s onwards. It came as a shock to the author when No. 4564 was transferred to Gloucester in September 1963 from St Blazey in Cornwall, where it had lain idle since April 1962. It survived here until September 1964, the final member of the 1,000-gallon type.

One of the 'push-pull' services is passing Naas Crossing running backwards at speed, on its way to Gloucester from Chalford and Stroud. The four tracks here comprise two in the foreground for the LMS Gloucester to Bristol line, and the two behind for the GWR Gloucester to Swindon route, the two running parallel to each other for about 6 miles to by Standish Junction. This had been something of a racing ground for years, and the famous locomotive driver J. W. Street, who joined the GWR in May 1891, mentions this in his autobiography. The departure times corresponded from Gloucester of the LMS 'Devonian' to Bristol and the GWR 'Cheltenham Flyer' (the one-time fastest train in the world) to Swindon and Paddington. Street says that he always gave the LMS train an initial advantage, but then overtook it and was never beaten. This was not just confined to the large express locomotives; the 'push-pull' services like this one on 2 November 1963 hauled by No. 1453 could reach 70 mph.

Left: The characteristics of the South Wales valleys meant that loaded heavy coal trains were worked downhill, allowing the use of small locomotives. For many years, 0-6-0s were used, but following the introduction of the 0-6-2 wheel arrangement in 1885 on the Taff Vale Railway, it came to be particularly associated with the area, with the extra water and coal capacity of the 0-6-2 being better matched to the work required. 0-6-2T No. 5677, built by the GWR in 1926, is seen on the northbound centre road at Gloucester Central in about 1964. One of the last steam sheds in the South Wales valleys was at Rhymney, and No. 5677 survived there until closure in March 1965, when it was transferred inter-regionally to Croes Newydd shed (6C) at Wrexham until withdrawal in the November. The August 1965 issue of the *Railway Observer* reported that cast iron cab-side number plates, similar to that on No. 5677, were available from the stores controller at Swindon for £1 plus carriage.

The Gloucester & Sharpness Ship Canal, that had its origins in the late eighteenth century, was built to avoid a narrow, winding, and dangerous section of the River Severn, and it enabled Gloucester to become an important inland port. The canal joined the River Severn at Sharpness, but after a new dock was built here in the 1870s that could accommodate ships too big for the canal, trade developed at Sharpness rather than Gloucester. Sharpness was connected to the Severn & Wye Joint Railway, warehouses were built, and the Sharpness New Dock & Gloucester & Birmingham Navigation Co. (until 1935) had their own railway and fleet of locomotives. This Avonside 0-4-0 W/N 1444 was built for the docks in 1902, the cab side number was originally SND No. 3, and became SD No. 3 in 1948, which was the number it kept under British Waterways management. The date of this photograph is unknown, but the locomotive was cut up on site in May 1964 by a Gloucester company.

Right: The branch from Kemble to Tetbury was authorised by Act of Parliament on 7 August 1884, and opened on 2 December 1889. Constructed by the GWR, it was 7 miles and 19 chains long, with originally only one intermediate station at Culkerton. The main station building here at Tetbury, in red brick with a tiled roof, was constructed during the First World War, and replaced the original wooden building. The small brick building in front served as the station stores-cum-bicycle shed. Diesel railbuses took over from steam in 1959, and there appears to be plenty of custom for unit W79978 on 3 August 1963, the seating capacity of which was forty-six passengers. The maximum speed allowed on the branch was 40 mph together with five restrictions between 15 and 25 mph. There were eight passenger trains each way daily from Monday to Friday in 1961, one extra on Saturdays, but none on Sundays. Tetbury closed to freight in July 1963, and for passengers in April 1964.

Above: The author's twelfth birthday present on 3 August 1963 was to spend the day on Talerddig Bank in Wales watching the all-steam activity. The diary of a friend with the author that Saturday refers to the weather as 'a dull Novemberish day'. Alan spent this day in Gloucestershire, where the weather was clearly similar, as GWR 'County' No. 1010 *County of Caernarvon* pulls into Kemble with what appears to be train 2B79, the 2.45 p.m. Gloucester to Swindon. Kemble was the junction station for the branches to both Cirencester and Tetbury. No. 1010 was another locomotive with a recent history similar to No. 4564 seen earlier at Gloucester; it had been at Plymouth in 1959, but following dieselisation, came north to a final home at Swindon. The water tower on the left had a booster tank mounted on top of it, the supporting structure for which can be seen in the photograph. In addition to feeding water columns here, it also supplied the GWR works at Swindon 13 miles away.

Earlier in this book at Worcester with No. 7025, mention was made of what has been described as one of the most epic rail tours of all time in terms of performance – 'The Great Western' high-speed 'Castle' hauled special from Paddington to Plymouth and return. Another of the reserve locomotives for this 9 May 1964 tour was Worcester-allocated No. 7022 *Hereford Castle*, and it is seen waiting on Swindon shed in case of problems. However, there were none on this part of the tour, and an average speed of 80.5 mph was maintained between here and Paddington. Alan was at Swindon on this day, having travelled on the Railway Correspondence & Travel Society's 'East Midlander No. 7' rail tour. Stanier 'Coronation' No. 46251 *City of Nottingham* hauled the tour from its namesake city to Didcot, where No. 46251 came off to go to Swindon for servicing. The tour carried on to Eastleigh Works, before making its way to Swindon, where No. 46251 took over again for the return to Nottingham.

Left, above and below: Photographed on the same day as those at Kemble and Tetbury, 3 August 1963, railbus W79976 arrives at Cirencester Town Station, and again as at Tetbury, there seems to be a healthy complement of passengers. Both the Cirencester and Tetbury branches were involved in an attempt to improve the economics of rural branch line passenger services. Lightweight railbuses of only 11 tons were built by AC Cars of Thames Ditton (the sports car manufacturer), and began service on both branches on 2 February 1959. It had been hoped to run them to and from Swindon, but their light weight could not be relied on to operate the track circuits, so connection was made at Kemble. Concurrently, three new halts were opened, and a fourth from 4 January 1960, plus a closed station was reopened. The new halts had ground-level platforms, were 25 feet long, and built of old railway sleepers. Retractable steps operated by the driver were fitted to the side of the railbuses, enabling passenger to enter and exit. The experiment proved a success, with the Cirencester branch carrying over 2,500 passengers a week in its first year, and although the corresponding Tetbury figure was only 10 per cent of this, it represented a 2.5x increase over the previous steam service. The Cirencester service was over-crowded at times, especially on Saturdays, plus it was difficult to carry the substantial mail and parcels traffic. Apparently, the record total was 110 passengers in a railbus with just forty-six seats. Despite all the early promise, passenger services on the Cirencester branch finished from 6 April 1964.

Alan had also visited Swindon the year before with the Stephenson Locomotive Society's 'Farewell to the Kings' tour of Sunday 28 April 1963. Photographed on Perutz colour film is one of the final GWR parallel-boiler pannier tanks built, No. 9666 from 1948. Actually built by the nationalised British Railways, it has just gone through the works and looks in excellent condition by the turntable, ready for return to traffic. It had come from one of the far-flung reaches of the GWR Empire, as indicated by the shed code on its smokebox of 87J Fishguard (Goodwick), and had been noted by the SLS monthly magazine in 'A' repair shop at Swindon on 17 March 1963. Fishguard shed closed in September 1963, and in the August, No. 9666 went to a new home in the South Wales valleys at Treherbert. Withdrawal came in September 1965 from Newport (Ebbw Junction) at virtually the close of BR steam operations in South Wales. No. 9666 met with the cutter's torch in Ward's scrap yard at Briton Ferry near Neath.

Following the Modernisation Plan of 1955, the Western Region of British Railways went its own way using diesel-hydraulic locomotives as opposed to diesel-electrics. This choice was based on advantages already recently proven in West Germany, such as a better power-to-weight ratio and a more compact design. The first true application of these principles in the UK was made in the D8xx 'Warship' class that weighed 78.6 tons for 2,070 hp, the diesel electric equivalent was the 'D2xx' class that weighed 133 tons for 2,000 hp, the 'Warships' being a compact four axle B-B design, whereas the 'D2xxs' had eight axles in a 1Co-Co1 arrangement. Pioneer class member D800 *Sir Brian Robertson* had entered traffic in August 1958, and was named after the chairman of the British Transport Commission from 1953 to 1961. This is another photograph taken at Swindon on 28 April 1963, this time in the works yard with Wendy Maund posing in front; D800 was withdrawn in October 1968.

The inside of 'A' shop at Swindon Works on 28 April 1963, and the change from steam to diesel is clearly visible. The order for D800, seen previously, was dated January 1956, and Swindon built thirty-eight of this class up to October 1961. D847 'Strongbow', seen here, was one of the Glasgow-built 'Warships', and while visually similar to D800, they were technically different internally. In September 1959, an order for a further class of diesel-hydraulics was placed, the D10xx 'Westerns', and thirty-five were scheduled to be built at Swindon. These are visible on the right of the photograph. The *Railway Observer* reported that on this date, D1019 to D1022 were complete, and that the frames had been laid down for D1023 to D1026. Nearest the camera is 'Hymek' D7050, only just over six months old, and possibly here to do with defects in the control block of the hydraulic transmissions causing malfunctioning of the gear shifts, which became a problem for the class in early 1963.

Undergoing repair inside Swindon works, again on 28 April 1963, is the first diesel-electric shunter purchased by the GWR in April 1936. It had been built the previous year by Hawthorn, Leslie & Co. under their W/N 3853, who made the frames and mechanical equipment, while the electrical gear was supplied by the English Electric Co. It was numbered '2' in the GWR stock, and was used at Acton for some years. Although during the Second World War it shunted the oil wharves at Swansea, after the war it returned to Acton, and became BR No. 15100 in February 1948. In its Great Western days, the body casing was painted green and lined out. No. 15100 had a maximum speed of 19 mph, when it could haul 500 tons on the level, at half this speed it could haul double the load, and on a gradient of 1 in 100 the maximum load was 750 tons at 2.7 mph. No. 15100 was withdrawn from Swindon shed in April 1965.

Above: No. 7027 *Thornbury Castle* was transferred to Worcester in April 1960, and this photograph is thought to date from that summer. The 'A22' headcode is that of the 'Cathedrals Express', so presumably No. 7027 is arriving at Worcester (Shrub Hill) with the Hereford portion of this at 8.45 a.m., the premier Paddington express on the route, and will join with the Kidderminster portion that has arrived a few minutes earlier at 8.42 a.m.; certainly the shadows being cast would tend to agree with this. The combined train was due to leave Shrub Hill at 8.55 a.m. with a scheduled arrival time in London of 11.25 a.m. In the right background can be seen the passenger side of Worcester shed, with a 'Modified Hall and '94xx' pannier tank visible outside. The small signal to the left of No. 7027, with 'BAY' written on it, controls the bay platform, used for some of the Bromyard branch services, on which we will soon travel as we journey south-west from Worcester.

This is Worcester (Foregate Street) Station with a 'Hymek' class diesel arriving on service 1A22, the up 'Cathedrals Express'. Close investigation of the 'Hymek's' number suggests that it might be D7076. The *Railway Observer*, in its July 1963 issue, reported that D7076 had been on loan from Old Oak Common shed in London to Worcester for crew training, and that this involved mainly two return journeys between Worcester and Hereford. It also understood that five 'Hymeks' would take over the rosters of Worcester's 'Castles'. The Worcester to Hereford line, whilst serving the main intermediate population centres of Malvern and Ledbury, was expensive to construct. The section from Rainbow Hill Junction to Henwick, including the station here, is mostly elevated on either substantial embankments or viaducts, and is about a mile in length. Today, although there are still two tracks at Foregate Street Station, they are operated as single lines, one from Henwick towards Tunnel Junction, and the other from Henwick to Shrub Hill.

Left: The engine shed complex at Worcester was surrounded by a triangle of railway lines, and in later years, this was used to turn steam locomotives rather than a turntable. Immediately to the right is the goods engine depot, with the coaling hoist and water tank also visible. The line that service 2V72 is standing on runs between Tunnel Junction and Rainbow Hill Junction and is 20 chains long. It allows services from the Birmingham direction to run directly towards Malvern, avoiding Shrub Hill station and the need to reverse. The tracks in the centre form the main running lines, to the right is a siding taken out of use in 1967, and that to the left is a running loop that became just a siding, also in 1967. This photograph is thought to date from the early summer of 1964 when service 2V72, hauled by a 'D75xx' series diesel, is listed in the Working Timetable as the 2.11p.m. Birmingham (New Street) to Worcester (Foregate Street).

No. 6679, a Stourbridge (2C) locomotive, has just descended the 1 in 132 gradient down to the River Teme floodplain, and is hauling the afternoon 'school train' from Worcester to Ledbury past what was left of Bransford Road Junction. When this junction was originally created, the signal box was known as Bromyard Junction, but when the branch was extended on to Leominster in 1897, it was changed to Leominster Junction, becoming Bransford Road Junction on 25 September 1950. The double-track connection to the Bromyard branch on the left, which had closed in September 1964 together with the signal box, was reduced to the one trailing point seen here on the up line to allow for dismantling trains in 1965. Judging from the vegetation, the photograph must date from around the summer of 1965, this service being one of the very last steam passenger workings from Worcester. Dieselising in the August, No. 6679 did not last much longer and was withdrawn a month later.

A pannier tank hauled train departs Suckley on its way from Bromyard to Worcester in about 1960. This is a rural area on the Worcestershire/Herefordshire border, and originally, the station had just a single platform and short siding. However, considerable fruit traffic developed with growers using Suckley as a railhead, and as trade grew, various alterations were made after 1899. First the siding was extended, and then in 1908, the up platform was extended, a crossing loop added along with a second platform and signal box. By 1956 things were in decline and the signal box closed, with three ground frames taking its place, the east of which is visible in the foreground. Both up and down services now used the up platform on the right. If it was necessary, services could still pass at Suckley, but not two passenger trains, and the train not conveying passengers had to be placed in the loop or sidings. All came to an end in September 1964 when the branch closed completely.

The Malvern Hills are the backdrop to this lovely September 1963 photograph taken from the down platform at Newland Halt. The unidentified 'Hymek' class diesel (the strange name being derived from its hydraulic Mekydro transmission) is hauling train 1A43, the four-coach 10.05 a.m. Hereford to Paddington, including one in chocolate and cream livery. In the 10 minute stop at Worcester (Shrub Hill), more coaches will be added before continuation to London. Newland Halt was one of many opened by the GWR in the inter-war years to combat expanding bus services, and in this example, March 1929. Previous to the Second World War, there were both up and down refuge sidings here, controlled by the continuously open signal box (because of Stocks Lane level crossing). During the war, a large permanent way depot was built at Newland to the right and behind the train, it was brought into use on 18 June 1943, and in 1963 was home to BR 0-6-0 service diesel locomotive No. PWM650.

Left, above and below: The story of the Bromyard branch was similar to many rural lines in this country, never really living up to expectations, and in the case here it took thirty-six years before it was possible to travel directly from Worcester to Leominster. The Worcester, Bromyard & Leominster Railway was incorporated by Act of Parliament in 1861, but was weighed down by financial problems and did not reach Bromyard until 1877. Leominster was reached in 1897, but the full 23¾ miles only stayed open until 15 September 1952 when the line was cut back to Bromyard. The length of time taken to construct the line is visible in the different building styles at Bromyard station, with the buildings on the right being those of the WBLR, while those on the left were built by the Leominster & Bromyard Railway and designed by William Clarke. No. 3682 was only transferred to Worcester shed (85A) in May 1964, and as the last normal service trains ran on Saturday 5 September 1964, the photograph clearly dates from the last weeks of the branch. No. 3682 is hauling the evening train from Worcester, and the lupins to its side are growing where a 150-feet section of the down platform was shortened in 1955. The view inside the cab on the same day shows evidence that No. 3682 was once allocated to Swindon (82C), and the driver is Alan's friend John Saunders. It remained at Worcester until the end of steam, and on the very last day, 31 December 1965, was noted on the shed and in steam with the legend 'best of the last' chalked on its cab side.

The difficulty of building the line from Worcester to Hereford has already been mentioned at Worcester (Foregate Street), and in addition, there were two tunnels plus a substantial viaduct west of Ledbury. Both the Malvern and Ledbury tunnels were built to a very narrow loading gauge, and although a new Malvern tunnel was built in the 1920s, this was never done at Ledbury. The photograph is taken at the north end of the Ledbury Tunnel, with a Worcester bound service in the mid-1960s climbing up the gradient that continues to Colwall. To the left can be seen a sand-drag, designed to stop runaway wagons etc. before getting on to the even steeper gradient in the tunnel. The yellow distant signal at danger by the entrance to the tunnel was controlled from Ledbury Station signal box. This was already electronically actuated by the early 1900s, and one of the first on the GWR, due to the conditions in the tunnel that caused problems with the usual manually-operated wire actuation.

The railway between Hereford and Worcester was a missing strategic link for the standard gauge. Prior to its opening in 1861, the only viable rail outlet for coal to London from South Wales was on Brunel's broad gauge via Gloucester, and this did not convert to standard gauge until 1872. At Ledbury on 26 October 1963, the route is still being used for the movement of South Wales coal, possibly one of the class 6 freight trains scheduled to leave Pontypool Road at 6.30 a.m. and 9.35 a.m. There was an uphill gradient of 1 in 80 through Ledbury tunnel, preceded by a short stretch of 1 in 70. A banking locomotive, in this case 2-8-0T No. 5245, was kept here for 144 hours per week specifically to help push heavy freight trains up the grade. Conditions in the restricted tunnel were unpleasant, and it has been described as one of the most foul in the country, so it was usual for the banking locomotive to assist working backwards.

Collett 0-6-0 '2251' class No. 2242 stands on the centre lines at Hereford, having worked a service from Gloucester (Central) via Ross-on-Wye in what is believed to be November 1963. This route was opened as broad gauge in 1855, but was one of the first to be converted to standard gauge in 1869. The passenger service ceased from 2 November 1964, as did freight traffic between Hereford and Ross. The '2251' class were ideal for light cross-country services, and in this era, Hereford shed (86C) had four allocated, including the only class member to be preserved, No. 3205. 0-6-0 tender engines had been used from the very early days of railways, with the Stockton & Darlington Railway acquiring the *Royal George* in 1827. Construction of the '2251s' began in 1930 and carried on into nationalisation, with the last two entering service in 1948. No. 2242 had entered service in 1945 and was withdrawn in May 1965; the last class survivor was withdrawn a month later.

Looking east from the up platform at Ross-on-Wye as another Hereford-allocated '2251' class, in this case No. 2286, arrives with a freight train from the Gloucester direction bound for Lydbrook Junction on 3 June 1964. The line to Lydbrook Junction was freight only at this time, and is being crossed by No. 2286. It was 5½ miles long and had originally been a through route to Monmouth, but passenger services were withdrawn in January 1959. The Ross-on-Wye station sign has had its 'change for Monmouth' wording painted over, and behind the sign is the bay platform that the Monmouth passenger service used. The quite substantial signal box opened in 1938 and replaced separate north and south boxes. Just visible above No. 2286 is the roof of Ross-on-Wye engine shed that had opened with the line to Gloucester in 1855, and so was built to take the wider broad gauge locomotives. Latterly, it was a sub-shed of Gloucester (Horton Road) (85B), but had closed in October 1963.

It is the summer of 1964, and GWR 'Mogul' No. 6349 is pulling away from Mitcheldean Road on a Hereford-bound train. The goods yard was on the right, but all the sidings had been removed in November 1963. The signal box closed when the passenger service ceased in November 1964, and for the next year of freight to Ross and Lydbrook there was no passing loop here, all trains using the up track to the left of No. 6349. A railway that has always intrigued the author started from this goods yard, the Mitcheldean Road & Forest of Dean Junction Railway, the Act for which was passed in 1871, with another in 1880 authorising the GWR to absorb the line and complete it. The section between Drybrook Quarry and Mitcheldean Road had track laid and was maintained by the GWR for over thirty years, but there was never any public traffic on it; this strange railway was taken up in the First World War for use elsewhere.

Left, above and below: GWR designed 'Large Prairie' 2-6-2 tank engine No. 4161 is seen in both of these photographs taken at Mitcheldean Road in 1964. The first is believed to have been taken on 27 May and the second on 6 April. The Gloucester to Hereford line was single track for the 21 miles and 37 chains between Grange Court and Rotherwas Junction, with passing loops to enable services to cross each other. To provide a safe method of working trains on single track lines, the token system was developed, and as No. 4161 arrives on a down service from the previous crossing station of Longhope, the fireman holds out the token for the section from there to Mitcheldean Road for the signalman, and at the same time collects the token for the next section on to Ross-on-Wye. On BR, the maximum speed for this in daylight was 15 mph, but there are stories of higher speeds where bruised arms could result. In the summer of 1962, the signal box opened at 6.00 a.m. and closed at 10.15 p.m. (10.35 p.m. on Saturdays) or whenever the last train had cleared. On Sundays, it was normally only opened if there were any engineering trains, or if the Severn Tunnel was closed when services such as the 11.00 a.m. Liverpool-Plymouth came this way. The maximum speed anywhere on the branch was 35 mph, and this applying to locomotives with axle loads of up to 17 tons 12 cwt. For the heavier 'red' locomotives, often used on the Sunday diversions, the maximum was 20 mph. The second photograph shows No. 4161 leaving bunker-first towards Gloucester.

Continuing from Hereford and Ross-on-Wye towards Gloucester, we arrive at Grange Court, a major junction where the main line from South Wales was joined. These views are both taken on 6 April 1964, the first showing the diverging routes to Ross (right) and South Wales (left), and the second of the junction station itself looking in the Gloucester direction. When construction of a railway to Ross was first mooted, it had been thought that owing to the difficulty of crossing the River Wye at Chepstow, it would form part of the main railway to South Wales via Monmouth. However, one of Brunel's major achievements was his Chepstow Bridge, and thoughts of an inland route to South Wales were abandoned in favour of today's route following the River Severn estuary. Making their way to South Wales scrap yards in the first photograph are four withdrawn locomotives, three class '2251s' and a pannier tank hauled by a Stanier '8F', a common sight at this time. In the up running loop is 2-6-0 No. 6349 on a mixed freight. This had been converted from a plain refuge siding to a loop with a sixty-five wagon capacity in December 1941. The signal box at this important junction was open continuously and had replaced two separate boxes in 1938, of which the west signal box used to stand just behind No. 6349. No. 6349 is seen again in the second photograph passing through the station on its way to Gloucester. Grange Court Station closed from Monday 2 November 1964, with the last trains calling on Saturday 31 October.

Retracing our steps, we now travel down the freight-only branch from Ross-on-Wye to Lydbrook Junction on 3 June 1964. Alan was lucky enough to get a ride on the footplate of No. 2286, arranged by the signalman in the photograph at Mitcheldean Road (p. 70). As mentioned at Grange Court, because of problems crossing the River Wye at Chepstow, it had been thought that the main line from London to South Wales would have to be constructed to the broad gauge along the route we are on here – Ross-Monmouth. North of Ross, the River Wye has the appearance of a mature river meandering across broad alluvial plains, but to the south, and particularly after Kerne Bridge where this sequence of photographs begins, incised meanders have formed looping gorges with steep sides. With little space for the railway, two bridges and two tunnels were required, and that at Symonds Yat expected to be particularly troublesome following trial borings. After overcoming the problem river crossing at Chepstow, the powers for a broad gauge line through Kerne Bridge lapsed. However, after a time it was resuscitated and promoted as a standard gauge line, and it opened from Ross-on-Wye to Monmouth (May Hill) in 1873. The first photograph shows No. 2286 about to leave Kerne Bridge, and to its left is a goods siding and loading gauge, while ahead in the middle-distance is the first crossing of the River Wye. Next, by the 4¾ mile post (from Ross-on-Wye), is the northern entrance to the 630 yards-long curving Lydbrook Tunnel, and finally the southern entrance filmed on the return journey. Interestingly, it is possible to walk through this tunnel today.

It is again 3 June 1964, and the branch freight has now reached Lydbrook Junction from Ross-on-Wye behind No. 2286. Up to 1959, there was a passenger service along the whole of the branch to Monmouth, but it was withdrawn from 5 January, and freight also ceased at the same time south of Lydbrook Junction to Monmouth (May Hill). The main reason for keeping this short branch open for freight can be seen behind the steam rising over the cab of No. 2286, the Edison Swan Cable Works, and some of the massive cable drums can be seen in the second photograph. Construction of the complex had started just before the First World War, and by the time war broke out, it was one of only four places in the country capable of producing braided electrical cables. Field telephone cabling was a speciality, and the floor space grew from an initial 540 square feet to 60,000 by 1919. The junction here was with the Severn & Wye Railway that descended from the Forest of Dean, a platform of which can be seen in the second photograph. The line up to the Forest lost its passenger service as early as 1929 and closed completely in early 1956, the tracks now just being used as sidings for about 30 chains. The small industrial diesel locomotive and wagons with rails on them are connected with the removal of the track that had remained in situ on the Monmouth section since 1959. The freight service continued until the last inbound train arrived behind No. 78006 on Friday 29 October 1965.

Coleford, in the Forest of Dean, had railway associations from very early on with the Monmouth Railway Act of 1810, although we would think of this as a horse-drawn tramway today. It eventually had two separate stations only a stone's throw apart, initially with no connection between them. Decline set in quite early, and in the First World War, much of the Monmouth line was taken up for war use. The other route to the east of Coleford lost its passenger service in 1929, but freight carried on until 1967, with a major source of traffic being Whitecliff Quarry. A connection between the two stations was opened, initially indirectly via adjacent sidings, but directly from 21 October 1951; importantly, this allowed easy access to the around 1 mile stub of the old Monmouth line that connected to the quarry. In the first photograph, pannier tanks Nos 3675 and 4689 have just worked across this 1951 link, and on 7 December 1965, taking empties to the quarry past Coleford GWR station. This was very near the end of steam working on the whole of the WR, with Gloucester shed, where both 3675 and 4689 were allocated, closing to steam at the end of the month. The next view is of the pair returning to Coleford. The maximum gradient back up this section was 1 in 44, which would limit a loaded train to around 200 tons per locomotive of this class, and these pannier tanks were the most powerful allowed. The stone trains carried on, diesel-hydraulic-hauled, until 11 August 1967 with both the 'D95xx' and 'D63xx' classes seeing service.

No. 45552 *Silver Jubilee*, so named because of the Silver Jubilee of HM King George V in 1935, looks in superb condition as it heads north out of Worcester (Shrub Hill), passing the locomotive shed to its left with the LCGB 'Thames, Avon, and Severn' rail tour of 12 October 1963. This was an ambitious tour that had started from London (Waterloo) at 9.02 a.m., initially heading for Woodford Halse on the Great Central line, then taking the SMJR to Stratford-upon-Avon Old Town before arrival at Worcester at 3.15 p.m., 30 minutes late. There can have been very few northbound departures, if any, from Worcester to Cheltenham involving a circular tour of Birmingham via both the Camp Hill and Bournville lines, but this is what *Silver Jubilee* is about to do. From Cheltenham 'Castle' *Sir Edward Elgar* took the train back to a 9.34 p.m. arrival at Paddington, and 94 minutes late, making a total mileage for the day of 352 miles and 54 chains.

Alan Maund and Wendy Waddoup married at Powick Parish Church, Worcester, on 11 August 1962. Their first and only home together was in Lower Town, Claines, not far from Fernhill Heath Station, so naturally, there is a large selection of photographs of this area to choose from as we now venture north from Worcester. The station was originally called Fearnall Heath, changing to Fernhill Heath in 1883. The photograph is dated September 1959, and shows two 'Cross-Country' DMUs coupled together on a through Birmingham (Snow Hill) to Cardiff General service. These ran via Kidderminster, Worcester (Foregate Street) avoiding Shrub Hill, and Hereford. Judging from the shadows, it is likely to be either the 8.00 a.m. or 10.00 a.m. departure from Birmingham, due to pass here about 50 minutes later, taking around 3.5 hours for the complete journey. This same type of DMU had taken over the other WR service from Birmingham to Cardiff via Stratford-upon-Avon on 10 March 1958, but did the journey about 30 minutes quicker.

Both these photographs of northbound freight trains were taken about half a mile from Fernhill Heath Station by the Strand Lane road bridge, and although undated, are probably from the summer months of 1963. The 'D65xx' diesel is hauling an oil train from the Fawley Refinery to Bromford Bridge, although steam in the form of 2-10-0s was initially used from the end of 1960 on this major contract for BR. To avoid congestion around Bristol, these services were by now routed via Eastleigh, Newbury, Didcot, Worcester, up the Lickey Bank, and Camp Hill before arrival at Bromford Bridge. The 'D65xxs' were based on the Southern Region, and in summer could be used on passenger trains, but not in winter, as they had no steam heating system. This paved the way for No. D6518 to be sent to Worcester for crew training in the wintery weather of January 1963, and by the May, the *Railway Observer* reported they had almost completely taken over the oil trains. These services were substantially loaded for the time, typically around 1,200 tons, and the train here looks to have tewnty-seven oil wagons that would weigh about 45 tons each. For safety reasons, buffer wagons were inserted between the locomotive and its train, this was strictly observed with fully loaded silver-painted tanks containing highly volatile products, but less so for empty silver tanks and for black-painted tanks used for low volatility products. The second photograph is of a typical mixed freight of the period, with a delightful mixture of wagons illuminated by the morning sun, and hauled by a GWR 'Prairie Tank'.

A short Class 9 pick-up freight is passing through Droitwich Spa Station towards Worcester on 11 September 1964 behind No. 6169, which has lost its smoke-box number plate, and gained instead a painted number on the buffer beam. There were a number of variants of these 'Large Prairies', all of which were visually quite similar, and this is the '61xx' class specifically constructed for the GWR suburban services around London; their higher boiler pressure allowing a faster acceleration. It was predicted that with early dieselisation of London suburban services, the class would be withdrawn soon after. However, this did not happen, and no fewer than thirty-one locomotives survived into 1965, the last full year of WR steam. Many were transferred away from London and relegated almost entirely to freight working. Worcester had four in November 1964, including No. 6169, the final member of the class to be built. In the previous November, it was allocated to Old Oak Common, London (81A). Looking in the other direction at Droitwich Spa is something that was always the cause of excitement amongst enthusiasts, a '9F' hauling a passenger train. Conventional wisdom had always been that freight locomotives with their smaller diameter wheels could not go fast, even some of the quite modern LMS 2-8-0s were restricted to just 40 mph. It seems to have been discovered around 1957 that these 2-10-0s could run fast and smoothly on a passenger train, and in August 1958 one reached 90 mph. The practice became frowned upon by authority, and No. 92128 will have no doubt achieved much more modest speeds in this undated photograph.

There is detail aplenty in this photograph at Droitwich looking north in about 1960 as a 'Modified Hall' approaches in the evening sunshine, taken from the bridge visible in the previous photograph here of No. 6169. In the middle distance is Droitwich Spa signal box. This controlled the junction of the routes to Kidderminster on the left and to Stoke Works Junction near Bromsgrove, which was the first to open on 18 February 1852 through from Worcester, on the right. The Birmingham & Gloucester Railway had bypassed both Worcester and Droitwich, but now with this OWWR line to Stoke Works being joined at Worcester to the existing OWWR line from Worcester to Abbots Wood Junction, a loop line had been created. The result was that all Midland Railway expresses (the successor to the B&GR) used this OWWR loop from the beginning. A curiosity was that, although some MR expresses called at both Droitwich and Worcester, passengers travelling just between the two were not allowed to use them.

With all the MR expresses going via Droitwich and Worcester on the 13 miles and 70 chains of loop line, the 11 miles and 20 chains of MR track from Stoke Works Junction to Abbots Wood Junction on the direct route saw little passenger traffic. A passenger service was maintained to the intermediate stations, but was little used, and withered away to just one stopping train each way daily before all the intermediate stations were closed at the end of September 1855. The result was something unusual in England for the next 100 years or so; a very long stretch of track, over 14 miles, with no intermediate passenger stations – from Bromsgrove to Wadborough. This undated photograph is taken close to one of these long closed stations, Spetchley, and shows class leader No. 92000 on a southbound oil train with no buffer wagons, possibly the 10.40 a.m. Bromford Bridge to Avonmouth as shown in the 1963 Working Timetable, due to pass here at around 12.15 p.m.

Approaching Bromsgrove from the south, on the quadruple track section in about 1960, is an unidentified but unnamed 'B1', hauling a substantial freight train that will clearly need banking assistance up the Lickey Incline. The 'B1s' were the LNER equivalent of the LMS 'Black Five' or the GWR 'Hall'. They were a mixed traffic locomotive mostly found on the Eastern and North Eastern Regions, plus the former LNER parts of the Scottish Region. The nearest allocation of 'B1s' that could work through Bromsgrove at this time was in the Sheffield area, and to cover their occasional visits south to Worcestershire and beyond, special instructions had been issued. The summer 1960 Working Timetable permitted their use as far as Gloucester (Eastgate), and if via the Worcester loop, a maximum speed of 20 mph was specified over the canal bridge (126 miles, 27 chains) at Droitwich. By 1962, this had been extended further south to both Bath (Green Park) and Bristol (Temple Meads), but again with the specific restriction at Droitwich.

Left, above and below: The outline of Stoke Works is visible in the haze of the first photograph; they are salt works founded in 1828. The track from Stoke Works to Bromsgrove was quadrupled in the early 1930s, and heading north up it is a 'Western' class diesel in an undated photograph. It is service 4E71, the 12.55 p.m. Margam to Frodingham and due to pass Stoke Works Junction at 5.07 p.m., one of two new direct trains each way first introduced on 15 July 1963, and a dedicated diesel-hauled freight service for steel industry traffic using the 'Westerns' offering a next-day arrival, the previous service occupied a number of days. Heading the other way appears to be a long, heavy, fully-loaded, loose-coupled, and non-automatic brake fitted coal train, which has just come down the Lickey Bank. This bank was famous for the fleet of locomotives used to push trains up it. However, coming down was a major problem for this sort of freight train, as the locomotive and its tender plus the guard's van on their own could not exert enough braking force to stop the train running away out of control downhill. The solution on all steep gradients was that at the top a percentage of the brakes on the wagons would be individually and manually pinned down to increase the braking force. At the bottom this procedure was reversed. The second photograph, also undated, shows a 'Peak' diesel heading south on the same four-track section. The four-character train identification of 1V36, shows it to be the 7.07 a.m. Bradford-Bristol, due to pass Stoke Works Junction at 11.18.5 a.m.

Moving up a mile or so brings us to Bromsgrove and the famous banking locomotives used for pushing heavy trains up the Lickey Bank. The gradient is 1 in 37.7 for 2 miles. It has been said that there are longer banks not as steep, and steeper banks not as long. From just after the First World War, one large banking locomotive plus numerous small 0-6-0 tank engines were allocated here to assist trains. Up to withdrawal in 1956, the large locomotive was 0-10-0 *Big Bertha*, but in 1956, its replacement in the first photograph arrived, '9F' 2-10-0 No. 92079; these large locomotives were regarded as the equal of two small 0-6-0s. Although the photograph is again undated, it is possible to narrow it down; No. 92079 is missing its headlight that was apparently removed about 1960, plus it was transferred to Birkenhead in October 1963. Looking at the hours of duty at Bromsgrove in the summer of 1960, No. 92079 was rostered for duty twenty-four hours a day and seven days a week! However, three time slots were shown for 'locomotive duties' viz. 9.10 a.m. to 10.00 a.m., 5.20 p.m. to 6.05 p.m., and 1.20 a.m. to 2.05 a.m. By the date of the second photograph January 1964, most of the 0-6-0s were GWR '94xxs', and these continued until the end of steam banking in September 1964, together with one '9F' 2-10-0. The number of bankers required largely depended on the weight of the train, and Bromsgrove's grandest sight, as seen here, was four for the very heaviest, which appears to be one of the loaded oil trains to Bromford Bridge.

Built at Swindon in 1963, these four-car 'Inter-City' units were designed to work from Cardiff to Derby and to Bristol, providing accommodation for 24 first-class and either 176 or 144 second-class passengers according to the composition of the unit. Pullman-type gangway connections were fitted at both ends of all vehicles, and the four-car units could be coupled together to form eight- or twelve-car sets, ten four-car sets were built. Their yellow front-end gangway cover together with wrap-round windows on either side of it made them visually very distinctive in the area, and in later years, they became the Class '123s'. The September 1967 issue of *Railway World* reported that one of the units was to act as test-bed for a Rolls-Royce 'Dart' gas turbine engine. The crowd at the end of the down platform at Bromsgrove are believed to be waiting for preserved No. 4472 *Flying Scotsman* to pass through, hauling a Festiniog Railway special from Retford to Cardiff on 18 March 1964.

The days of hauling express passenger trains up and down the main line from Bristol to Birmingham and beyond have finished now for LMS 'Jubilee' No. 45682 *Trafalgar*. It is October 1963, and although No. 45682 is still allocated to the same shed as in the all-steam days of 1959, Bristol (Barrow Road) (82E), the nearest it normally gets to passenger work now are the local stopping services along its old stomping ground. The steep gradient of the Lickey Bank can be seen behind, as No. 45682 draws to a halt at Bromsgrove with possibly either the 4.40 p.m. or 5.25 p.m. Birmingham (New Street) to Gloucester (Eastgate) stopper. To the right are Bromsgrove Works that had been established as the maintenance facility for the B&GR and a couple of locomotives were actually built here in the early days. By 1963, it was a wagon works and had been for many years. They closed in September 1964 following a review of railway workshops published on 19 September 1962.

Climbing the Lickey Bank with impressive smoke and steam effects is a BR Standard Class 5 4-6-0. The load appears to be eight coaches, well over the maximum allowed unaided up the bank of 190 tons tare weight for this class, which would translate to five or possibly six coaches depending on the stock. However, there is no steam or smoke coming from the banker, so this is likely to be after diesels took over in September 1964. The single headlamp on the top of the smoke box indicates a class 2 passenger train, the same as in the previous photograph with No. 45682, and so this is probably one of the local stoppers in the period from September 1964 until the service ceased at the beginning of January 1965. The 7.33 a.m. from Gloucester could load to eight coaches and would pass here at around 9.15 a.m. All this, together with no leaves on the trees and the low sun, probably means the photograph dates from about December 1964.

About 1½ miles towards Birmingham from the top of the Lickey Bank is Barnt Green. The B&GR opened through here in 1840, although the station did not open until 1844, and it became a junction in 1859 when the branch diverging to the right opened to Redditch. The railway was quadrupled from Barnt Green north to Halesowen Junction, opening on 25 May 1930. This magnificent panorama dates from about 1960, and shows MR 4F 0-6-0 No. 43940 from Saltley shed (21A) heading towards Bromsgrove with a freight. From 1 February 1958, the regional boundary between the WR and LMR was moved to the up distant signals south of Barnt Green on both the main and Redditch lines. The passenger warnings signs at the end of the platform are still in WR brown, despite now being in LMR territory. The sidings and pointwork etc. remained largely intact until the end of the 1960s when rationalisation occurred, including the closure of Barnt Green signal box in April 1969.

Another line involved in the 1 February 1958 boundary changes was that from Halesowen Junction through Rubery to the down distant signal at Halesowen (WR); all this now became LMR territory. The signal box at Rubery shows the line's MR heritage, and it opened in 1883, but an Act of 1906 made it a joint line between the MR and GWR, nevertheless, despite this the passenger service was exclusively MR until its withdrawal in April 1919. The opening of the Austin Motor Company works at Longbridge increased traffic considerably and a workmen's passenger service was introduced. The branch was single track, had long stretches of 1 in 50 gradients, sharp curves, and a fragile 234 yards long viaduct at Dowery Dell, yet in 1958 there were fourteen scheduled workings in each direction. The viaduct restricted the locomotives allowed over it, and explains the survival of MR Johnson '2Fs' that had their origins as far back as 1875. No. 58138 has a Saltley (21A) shed plate below its smoke box number and was allocated there in February 1960, where it stayed until reallocated to Toton (18A) in December 1961. It is also seen in the second photograph at Hunnington, with one of the station's ground frames visible on the right. In the photograph at Rubery, '4F' No. 43975 is also present shunting; the '4Fs' were heavier locomotives and could not work over the central section of the line that included the viaduct. The section of line from the Longbridge works through Rubery and Hunnington to Halesowen was closed in 1964.

Stourport Power Station was built by the Shropshire, Worcestershire, & Staffordshire Electric Power Co., a 32 acre site had been found at the head of navigation of the River Severn and close by the Staffordshire & Worcestershire Canal, allowing for coal delivery by boat/barge and a supply of cooling water. Work began in 1923, and the first supplies - to neighbouring Kidderminster were provided on 1 April 1926. The power station was officially opened by Prime Minister Stanley Baldwin on 2 June 1927. As demand grew and grew, so it was expanded, until in the Second World War a second power station was authorised (Stourport B) that was officially opened on 26 September 1950. By the middle of the 1950s, capacity was 300,000 kW. In 1940, a connection from the power station was made to the Severn Valley branch of the GWR, and at the end of the war, coal deliveries by canal ceased. All of the railway system seen in these undated photographs was elevated on a concrete lattice gantry, the first of which shows Andrew Barclay W/No. 2088 of 1940 and named after director Sir Thomas Royden. In the second photograph is another 0-4-0, a Peckett built in Bristol W/N 1893 of 1936, which arrived at Stourport in the 1950s. The locomotives spent their time bringing full wagons to the coal tipplers, as in the first photograph, and then taking the empties back to the exchange sidings. This was the last use in Worcestershire of steam locomotives commercially.

Alan decided to make one final journey along the Severn Valley line to Shrewsbury before it closed as a through route at the end of the summer timetable in September 1963. The British weather looks to be at its best, as a single-car DMU approaches Bewdley in the early afternoon of a June Saturday in 1963. As a young boy, the author had been surprised by the amount of dieselised passenger trains at Bewdley early on in the diesel era; even in 1959 it was possible to see three such services all here at the same time. As passenger traffic was not normally heavy, the GWR railcars introduced from 1940, specifically to improve the economics of rural branch lines, had been a common sight for years around Bewdley. By 1963 however, all the GWR units had been withdrawn and their place taken by ones similar to that arriving, displaying 'Shrewsbury' in the small destination indicator above the centre cab window. At the other end of the station in monochrome, also heading up the Severn Valley line, is class leader No. 82000, which was allocated to Shrewsbury from November 1955 to February 1959. These locomotives were built because of the existence of a number of bridges having a 16-ton weight restriction. The entire class were built at Swindon with No. 82000 entering service in April 1952 at Tyseley. Interestingly, the locomotive diagram for this engine lists its maximum axle load as 16 tons 8 cwt. No. 82000 survived until December 1966, probably because it had a major overhaul including a boiler change in October 1963.

The GWR railcars referred to previously could be seen on all four branches radiating from Bewdley, and this one is arriving at Cleobury Mortimer whilst working from Tenbury Wells to Bewdley. The station at Cleobury Mortimer was over a mile away from the town, and much of this line passed through a very rural area on the Worcestershire/Shropshire border. It was no surprise when 'normal' passenger services were withdrawn from 31 July 1961. However, principally for the use of schoolchildren, a service of one train a day (Monday to Friday) was maintained at 7.55 a.m. from Tenbury Wells to Kidderminster, returning at 4.10 p.m., but this too succumbed at the end of July 1962. Freight carried on at Cleobury Mortimer until the spring of 1965, because of the branch from here to Ditton Priors where there was a Royal Navy Armaments Depot.

Travelling further along the route from Bewdley and Cleobury Mortimer we arrive at Woofferton Junction, where it connected to the main line between Shrewsbury and Hereford. A letter to the editor of *Railway Magazine* in December 1961 from a Mr J. A. Best of Rugeley, recalled a family visit to the station some thirty years previously when the names on the platform name-board, signal box, and platform luggage trolleys were spelt in three different ways viz. Woofferton, Wofferton, and Wooferton. This view at Woofferton Junction (this is the correct spelling!) dates from around 1960, and is looking south as a DMU arrives from Hereford. In the down platform is Kidderminster allocated 'Large Prairie' No. 4175 that has worked a train in from the Bewdley branch. The sign on the right attached to the footbridge, and also another between No. 4175 and the DMU, showed the stopping position for particular DMU-car lengths. The finger boards on the up side station buildings indicated destinations of the various services.

Taken on Alan's return June 1963 journey from Shrewsbury, he had changed trains at Bridgnorth, and this is the last but one southbound service of the day on the approach to Hampton Loade ('loade' derives from an old word for river crossing), with the points set to take the single-car DMU into the up platform. The scheduled arrival time is 6.56 p.m., and a northbound train, again a single-car DMU, will be passed here. South of Hampton Loade on the 2 miles and 12 chains section to Highley was Alveley Colliery Halt, which was not shown in the public timetable. When the Severn Valley line was shut by BR in September 1963 as a through route, it was kept open from the south for freight to Alveley Colliery until 1969, when it too closed. Today, and largely thanks to the efforts of enthusiasts and volunteers, the railway has been restored as the Severn Valley Railway from Bridgnorth to Kidderminster, with the first section to Hampton Loade opening in 1970.

Right: Further up the Severn Valley is Coalport, which had stations on both banks of the river. The Severn Valley line station was on the west bank, but this is the London & North Western Railway station on the east side being dismantled during April 1962. Coalport had been developed as a 'new town' in the early days of the Industrial Revolution, around 1794, the idea being to build an inland port on the River Severn and Shropshire Canal, to ship products from the East Shropshire coalfield downriver to Gloucester and Bristol in the famous shallow-draught 'Severn Trows'. Although initially successful, the canal suffered from subsidence caused by the coal mines. An Act of 1857 authorised the LNWR, by then owners of the canal, to build a railway from Hadley near Wellington to Coalport using parts of the canal bed. In latter years, this steeply-graded branch saw little passenger traffic, and it ceased from 2 June 1952, the freight service following on 5 December 1960.

Above: For some years previously to this June 1963 photograph at Bridgnorth, the only regular steam passenger services on the route had all been workings from the Shrewsbury end. Looking in the public timetables for both 1958 and 1963, it was generally possible to tell if they were steam or diesel; the diesel services usually having a '2' at the top of the relevant column, because both the GWR railcars and their BR successors only had second class accommodation. Of the five services from Shrewsbury to Bridgnorth in the summer 1958 timetable, four were steam-hauled, but south from here of the eight trains listed, only one was steam, and this with a locomotive that had started from Shrewsbury. Ivatt 2-6-2T No. 41209 has worked the last service of the day from Shrewsbury and will leave in about one hour on the last northbound train. A single-car DMU arrived from and departed to the south at similar times to give connections along the whole length of the line.

Alan has labelled this view as Shifnal Bank in September 1962 with 'King' No. 6027 *King Richard I*, and although the locomotive's headboard says the 'Cambrian Coast Express' the reporting code 'Z28' indicates a special train. The last regular employment of the 'Kings' was on the augmented service from Paddington to the West Midlands, while the LNWR route from Euston was electrified, and their use on this largely ceased with the introduction of the winter timetable on 10 September 1962. No less than thirteen 'Kings' were withdrawn in the September, nearly half of the class, including No. 6027. A deterrent to using the heavy 'Kings' west of Wolverhampton was the condition of Shifnal Viaduct, and this was reconstructed between 18 October and 29 November 1953. Nevertheless, 'Kings' on Shifnal Bank remained unusual for some years, and *Trains Illustrated* could report that on 1 January 1959, for only the second time, a 'King' hauled the 'Cambrian Coast Express' in both directions on the same day. Today, although the railway is still open, Alan would find the view virtually unrecognisable, with the industrial buildings of Stafford Park, Telford, dominating the scene.

Left, above and below: These two views are of Madeley Junction between Wellington and Shifnal, the first was taken on 21 March 1966 and the second on 2 May 1966. The 'Warship' heading east is D859 *Vanquisher*, one of the Glasgow-built variety, and is displaying code 1V19, of which the 'V' indicates a train bound for the WR and probably Paddington via Birmingham (Snow Hill), a rare class to see here in the author's experience. In 1967, following the change to semi-fast trains from Paddington to Birmingham (New Street) this class was used for a while, and the *Railway Observer* reported crew training on them taking place in the spring of 1967 through Madeley Junction. Confirming Alan's 1966 date, the crossover in front of D859 had been removed by the time of the engineering work going on in the second photograph, replaced by the new one on the other side of the bridge from which both slides were taken. The signal box behind D859 was replaced by a new one between the main line and the branch on the left, which will see 'merry-go-round' coal trains running through to Ironbridge Power Station. Workmen are busy with track-work as 2-10-0 No. 92228, a Banbury allocated locomotive since its entry to service in July 1958, passes them by with two very interesting wagons at the head of its train. These are Special Cattle Vans (SCVs), and used for shipping prize cattle together with room for an accompanying drover. They appear to be the six-wheeled variety constructed after the Second World War, and the number of the first seems to be W759W.

If there was such a thing as a universal type of locomotive in the last days of steam, then a good candidate would surely be the Stanier 'Black 5' or its BR equivalent. Passing the continuously open No. 2 signal box at Wellington (Salop) on one of the two centre-roads avoiding the station platform tracks, is the BR development of the 'Black 5'. The two lamps on the left of the buffer beam show this to be an express freight, pipe-fitted throughout with the automatic vacuum brake operative on not less than 90 per cent of the vehicles. No. 73095 had been constructed at Derby and entered traffic in November 1955 in black livery at Manchester. It came to Shrewsbury in September 1958 where it stayed for nearly seven years. As can be seen, No. 73095 was one of the class members to be painted green, and done at Doncaster in 1960 – and very smart it looks on No. 73095, bathed in the evening sun in another undated photograph.

Right: Alan had only about 1.5 hours at Shrewsbury in June 1963 before heading back to Bewdley. Passing through is this unidentified 'County' on a class 8 unbraked freight that appears to include some wagons loaded with ironstone, possibly bound for the steel works at Brymbo. For your author in Worcestershire, these were rare locomotives, as the class of thirty tended to keep to the outer reaches of the old GWR Empire at such places as Penzance, Neyland, and Shrewsbury. In February 1963, Shrewsbury shed had six, but by the end of the year all had either been withdrawn or reallocated. This example, although missing its smoke box number plate, is displaying an 89A shed code that was the WR code for Shrewsbury, and after this area was transferred from the WR to LMR at the beginning of 1963, the shed code became 6D. In the middle distance is Severn Bridge Junction signal box, which in 2011 became the largest operational mechanical signal box in the world.

Above: The engine shed at Wellington was situated just to the north of the station, from which this undated photograph was taken. The date of construction is uncertain, and could be as early as 1849 by the Shrewsbury & Birmingham Railway. However, it was reported that in 1876, a goods shed was to be converted by the GWR for the purpose of stabling both their own and LNWR locomotives, this enabling the GWR to work over certain LNWR lines. It was a three-road shed measuring 50 feet by 85 feet, and on nationalisation had an allocation of seventeen locomotives, mostly for local work such as the Much Wenlock and Craven Arms branch, plus trips to nearby collieries. On view are pannier tank No. 3792 and diesel-shunter D3028, both of which were Wolverhampton-based in the early 1960s. After transfer to the LMR in 1963, the shed code became 2M, and it closed in August 1964. Today the site is used as a car park for the railway station.

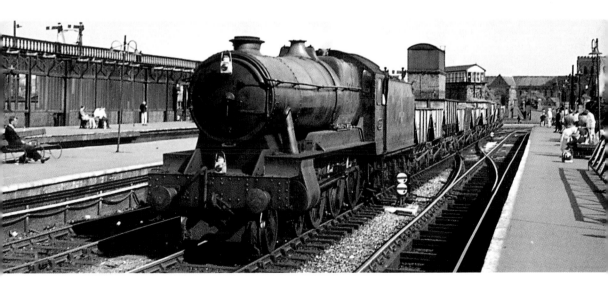

In a photograph believed to date from March 1962, this is what was left of the Snailbeach District Railways. This was a narrow gauge line (2 feet 3¾ inches) that opened in 1877, and it connected the Stiperstone Mines, with an exchange siding on the Minsterley branch at Pontesbury in south-west Shropshire. The earthworks of this steeply graded line with a ruling gradient of 1 in 37 were of sufficient size to allow conversion to standard gauge. By the First World War, things were in a parlous state. However, Colonel Stephens took over on 1 January 1923, and repairs and improvements were embarked upon. In 1944, the *Railway Magazine* reported trains ran only three days a week, with locomotive haulage of the empties to the quarry, as gravity was used on the descent. Steam operation lasted until the summer of 1946, and thereafter, a Fordson tractor was used. By 1955, it was reported that only six wagons were in running condition, and in 1962, the final lengths of track were removed.

A very presentable BR Standard Class 2 No. 78030 simmers away at Crewe North in September 1963, the shed to which it was allocated from 1956 to 1964. It seems to have led something of a pampered life and was normally kept very clean, as in addition to local station pilot and shunting duties, No. 78030 was used on officers' specials and inspection saloon work, and in June 1963, was noted on such duties at Harlech. The giant structures in the background are two ash-removal plants, and on the right, an automated coaling tower, an indication of the investment made by the LMS to reduce the labour costs of servicing steam locomotives. In contrast to the GWR, with their soft Welsh coal that needed delicate manual handling, the LMS used hard coal that could be dropped from mechanical coaling plants. Tests done at the Nine Elms (London) automated coaling plant with Welsh coal by Harold Holcroft showed that 19 per cent of it ended up as dust and fine particles.

The first of the British Railways Standard locomotives to appear in January 1951 were the 'Britannias', and in total fifty-five were built in three batches, with the last entering traffic in September 1954, their boilers being regarded as the pinnacle of British design. BR Executive Officer (design) E. S. Cox decided that essential features would be simplification of construction and provision of good accessibility to parts needing maintenance to minimise the work of servicing and repair. But there were many enthusiasts who looked at the 'Britannia's' outward appearance in horror, with their angular looks and high running plate. Initially, the class were spread about with examples allocated in England, Scotland, and Wales. However, by around 1964, the time of these photographs, all were on the LMR. No. 70015 *Apollo* had been on the WR for many years, and still has its red route availability disc as evidence of this below the cab side number, and it is seen on Crewe North (5A) shed. The spaces in the smoke deflector are hand-holds, fitted following the derailment of No. 70026 in 1955 to improve driver visibility. No. 70004 *William Shakespeare* is seen by the south end of Crewe station and still has the fixing bolts on its smoke deflector for working the 'Golden Arrow' express from London to Dover, and also the original smoke deflector hand rail. No. 70004 was also the final steam locomotive to be repaired at Darlington works. Both locomotives ended their days at Carlisle Kingmoor (12A) in 1967, which was a final home to many 'Britannias'.

Your author has always felt that the 'Electric Blue' livery of the West Coast Main Line electric locomotives suited them exceptionally well, and in another photograph taken at Crewe in September 1963, E3004 is displaying this livery. The adoption of 25kV ac, instead of 1.5 kV dc that was originally intended to be the standard, required greater clearances from line electrical equipment to both fixed structures and the train. Research was done at Crewe using a steam locomotive underneath a bridge to measure the distance electrical flashover occurred. In 1961, the Ministry of Transport agreed to a reduction from 11 to 8 inches, and in addition, it was decided to reduce the loading gauge from 13 feet 6 inches to 13 feet 1 inch. These two reductions enabled the Euston-Crewe-Liverpool-Manchester electrification scheme to use 25 kV throughout more easily and economically. Dual-voltage 6.25 kV/25 kV ac had been used elsewhere, such as with the Glasgow 'Blue Trains', this allowing reduced clearances in built-up areas with the trains having voltage detection and transformer changeover equipment on them.

The LMS were early pioneers of diesel shunting locomotives, and following the trial of eleven locomotives, decided that around 350 hp was essential for intensively used yards, plus that electric transmission was the only one sufficiently developed for such amounts of power. In 1934, Charles Fairburn joined the LMS as Electrical Engineer, coming from English Electric, and in 1935, orders were placed for ten diesel-electrics from both Armstrong Whitworth and English Electric. It was from the latter that the standard LMS shunter was evolved, with the first forty built from 1939, having jackshaft drive, including No. 12011, seen here at Crewe South in about 1963. Thereafter, the more elegant arrangement of two nose-suspended motors driving the axles direct through double reduction gearing was worked out, and shunters following these principles are still at work today. The economics were overwhelmingly in favour of these 350-hp shunters, and on duties rostered for 6,000 hours per annum there was a 45 per cent saving in costs over steam. No. 12011 was withdrawn in March 1966.

At the end of 1947, the LMS embarked on a major experimental programme involving the final 100 'Black Fives'. The aim was to improve locomotive availability and reduce maintenance costs, the first fruit being fitting ten locomotives with roller bearings, which required an increase of 4 inches in the wheelbase between the two rear axles, with the revised figure then being applied to all later new 'Black Fives'. Seen at Crewe South on 9 August 1964 following withdrawal, No. 44738 comes from the next experiment in 1948 with twenty locomotives. All were equipped with Caprotti poppet valve gear, but ten had roller bearings while the other ten, including No. 44738, had plain bearings. Although the Caprotti valve gear was an aesthetic disaster, it gave little trouble and reduced maintenance costs. While free-running at speed, they were weaker on banks, and on the climb to Fishponds from Bristol (Temple Meads) had a load limit of 30 tons, or about one coach, below that of a standard 'Black Five'

We have already seen the GWR 0-6-0 design that became their standard shunting and general purpose tank engine, the LMS equivalent, and seen on Crewe South (5B) shed in about 1963, was the 'Jinty'. The design had its origins in a Midland Railway design by S. W. Johnson of 1899, of which sixty were built. After the Grouping of the railways, the LMS continued building the class, and another 422 were constructed between 1924 and 1930. No. 47530 was from the LMS series, but was built by William Beardmore & Co. of Glasgow in 1928. Prominent on No. 47530's water tank is an electrification warning sign. Many tracks around Crewe were already fitted with 25 kV ac overhead cables, and there had been examples of injury, or worse, to staff climbing on locomotives. No. 47530 came to 5B in October 1961, and was withdrawn from the same shed five years later. A few examples survived into 1967 and nine of the class have been preserved, not including No. 47530.

By the turntable at Crewe South in September 1963 is the result of another locomotive experiment, this time in the quest of greater efficiency. Coal savings in excess of 20 per cent had been reported in Italy using the Franco-Crosti system, which enabled the maximum amount of heat to be extracted using a preheater from that liberated in the locomotive's firebox. Ten locomotives were built by BR in 1955 using the slightly different Crosti system, due to limitations of the British loading gauge. When tested, the savings were found to be minimal or non-existent, yet maintenance costs were much higher due to severe corrosion. By 1958, the experiment was over and a conversion programme was started to alter the locomotives to conventional operation. No. 92024 was converted in early 1960, and its clean appearance in the photograph is presumably because of a light casual repair at Crewe works between 27 August and 20 September 1963. No. 92024 was withdrawn in November 1967 from Birkenhead shed (8H).

Right, above and below: The electrification of the West Coast Main Line proceeded southwards towards London, with electric working being extended by the LMR on 2 March 1964 from Stafford to Nuneaton. This section including Rugeley (Trent Valley) where these two photographs are taken, both of which date from the mid-1960s. The intention of the electrification programme was to push on to Euston and leave the Birmingham lines till last. After testing, the first electrically hauled train out of Euston was the 8.35 a.m. to Liverpool on Monday 22 November 1965. The first photograph shows E3073 on a southbound freight, a member of class 'AL5' (later class '85'), while the second is of class 'AM4' four-car multiple-unit No. 044 (later class '304'), one of the final batch constructed specifically for use on the Crewe to Rugby section. Despite the extensive works and costs involved in electrification, the economics work out very favourably, and these were presented at a conference of the Institution of Electrical Engineers in October 1968. Comparing the 1965-built main line electric (class '86') and diesel locomotives (class '47') over 25 years, the annual capital charges for the electric were 77 per cent of the diesel's. Maintenance and fuel costs for the electric, including that of the overhead cables in the case of the electric locomotive, were 74 per cent of the diesel's costs. It was the presentation of this paper that made a clear case for extending the electrification northwards to Glasgow. Incidentally, it was noted that where steam locomotives had been eliminated, the carbons on the pantographs used for taking electricity from the overhead cables had over four times the life.

Although steam on BR was fast disappearing by the mid-1960s, it was still possible to see locomotives at industrial sites about the country, and in particular the National Coal Board. In fact, after the total demise of BR main line steam, the largest operator nationally became the NCB. These three photographs are all taken on a snowy Saturday 6 March 1965 around the Cannock Chase area, where coal mining had been carried out from as early as the thirteenth century. A celebrity locomotive is seen at Hednesford in the photograph above left; this is *Cannock Wood*, which had been built by the London, Brighton & South Coast Railway in 1877. It was purchased from the Southern Railway in 1927, and after decades more use in the Cannock area, it was preserved by the Railway Preservation Society in the 1960s. CRC stands for the Cannock & Rugeley Colliery Company. The photograph above right shows *Hanbury*, which was built by Peckett in 1894 W/N 567; the Hanbury family were among the pioneers of coal mining in South Staffordshire. The photograph below is taken at Littleton Colliery. The rail link from here connected with the Wolverhampton to Stafford main line close by Penkridge, and passed underneath the M6 Motorway. The nearest locomotive is *Holly Bank No. 3*, built by Hunslet in 1924 with a Works Number of 1451, and behind it is *Robert Nelson No. 4*, another Hunslet from 1936 W/N 1800. At its peak, Littleton Colliery employed more than 2,000 people and produced over a million tons of coal annually. When it closed in 1993, it was the last deep mine in Staffordshire.

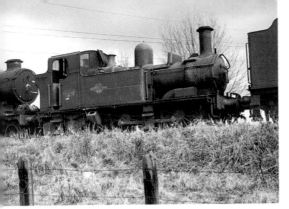

Until about the end of the 1950s, the railway's own workshops would often cope with the cutting up of withdrawn locomotives, but due to both the change from steam power and a contraction of business done by the railways, so many were being condemned that private contractors started being used in addition. One such contractor was John Cashmore Ltd, and we see a sad GWR 0-4-2T No. 1424 ready to begin its last journey to their scrapyard at Great Bridge, Tipton, in the first photograph. The second locomotive is believed to be 0-6-0PT No. 5420, and if it was not for the fact that its number plates are missing, you could think that this otherwise well-presented engine was ready for another day's work, although it is in fact destined for Cooper's Metals Ltd at California Siding, Sharpness. Lined green livery became standard for this class from the late 1950s, and although it has the correct yellow circle indicating its route availability on the cab-side, the power classification of 'C' inside the circle is incorrect, as these locomotives were in the ungrouped power class. The third photograph shows a row of entirely GWR locomotives, and prominent is '2251' class No. 3203. This met with the cutter's torch a very long way from GWR territory at A. King & Sons Ltd of Norwich. All three locomotives had a final working home at Gloucester, and all were withdrawn towards the end of 1963. A clue to their location is the GWR ¾ mile post in the last photograph, and this is believed to be on the GWR Gloucester Docks branch from Over Junction to Llanthony.

Also in the West Midlands is Bescot, and this became a final home to the last members of a very successful class of locomotives, the legendary 0-8-0 'Super Ds'. The origins of these locomotives is complex, with the earliest examples on the LNWR dating from Victorian times, and many were rebuilt, some a number of times over the years. No. 49430 is a member of class 'G2', and had been constructed at Crewe in 1922. Uniquely for LNWR 0-8-0s, the 'G2s' were not rebuilt from or into other classes. Simple, robust, and powerful, they were superior to their replacements the LMS 0-8-0s, whose boiler repair costs were 50 per cent higher. On nationalisation of the railways in 1948, there were 478 LNWR type 0-8-0s still in use. This photograph was taken on 27 October 1963, at which time only six were left in service, all in the West Midlands. The final examples, including No. 49430, were withdrawn in the four weeks ending on 26 December 1964.

Although regarded by some as the ugliest locomotives ever to have operated in Britain, the Ivatt class '4MT' 2-6-0s were the result of a great deal of thought. They were seen as the long-awaited replacement of the '4F' 0-6-0s, whose design dated back to 1911. Examples of key points in the design were: two outside cylinders; fabricated components for ease of manufacture; exposed pipework for ease of fitting and repair; high running boards for ease of access to boiler fitments; an inset coal bunker on the tender to allow better vision whilst working backwards. The result, rather inevitably, was a very utilitarian design with a controversial appearance. Initially, No. 43022 had an enormous double chimney, making it look even more bizarre. The class proved to be a reliable workhorse, and once their steaming problems were cured with a newly designed single chimney, they formed the basis of the BR '76xxx' class. No. 43022 stands close to the automated coaling tower at Bescot shed in November 1963.

The largest and most powerful class of locomotives on the GWR were the 'Kings', thirty of which were built between 1927 and 1930. The 'Castle' class, as seen previously in this book, numbered over five times as many and were built between 1923 and 1950. One reason so many more 'Castles' were built compared to 'Kings' was the heavier axle-load of the bigger locomotive – 22.5 tons compared to 19.7 tons – and this restricted the 'Kings' to routes such as Paddington to Wolverhampton or Plymouth. 'Kings' never appeared (pre-preservation) at Worcester. The reality in the 1950s was even worse; changes such as heavier section wheel centres, stiffened up frames, plus larger and heavier superheater headers had pushed the axle-load up to a maximum of 25 tons. All the 'Kings' had been withdrawn by the end of 1962. However, one was specially returned to service, No. 6018 *King Henry VI*, to haul this special train on 28 April 1963 from here at Birmingham (Snow Hill) to Swindon and back.

Birmingham (New Street) was built as a joint station by the LNWR and MR between 1846 and 1854, replacing earlier termini in the city, and when completed, it had the largest iron and glass roof in the world. Due to increasing congestion, the MR built a second train shed, and the two combined covered some 14.5 acres, of which 8 acres were roofed. In 1900, between 8.00 a.m. and 12 p.m., forty trains per hour were arriving and departing, reaching a peak of fifty-three between 8.00 a.m. and 9.00 a.m. This view is thought to date from 8 September 1957, with Nos 42337 and 40332 standing in the MR section, while on the right in the LNWR part, now without its impressive roof, stands an unidentified '2P' 4-4-0. Congestion has become a problem again, with passenger usage up by over 50 per cent between 2005 and 2010, and a redevelopment is underway. However, the track and platform levels at Birmingham (New Street) are to remain largely unchanged.

It is Tuesday 7 April 1964, and coming from the Birmingham direction is 'Castle' No. 7026 *Tenby Castle* on a parcels train, about to pass under Station Road bridge by Hatton South Junction. To the right of No. 7026 note the mile post, indicating 112¼ miles from Paddington via Oxford, while curving away to the left is the branch to Stratford-upon-Avon. By this time there was little passenger work for No. 7026, although in the summer of 1964 it would find employment on Saturday holidaymaker services, with withdrawal in the autumn. The train could be the 8.42 a.m. Shrewsbury to Paddington parcels train via Oxford, and due to pass Hatton at 3.39 p.m. Immediately to the left of No. 7026 and in the middle of the adjacent track, is part of the GWR Automatic Warning System. This had been developed in the early years of the twentieth century, and if a signal was passed at danger, these ramps could use electromagnets to automatically apply the brakes.

Left, above and below: Despite the poor light conditions inside Tyseley locomotive depot on what is believed to be 31 January 1965, the subject of the first photograph is unique – the last steam locomotive to be built by British Railways. No. 92220 had been built at Swindon and entered service following a special ceremony on 18 March 1960, where it was named *Evening Star*. On the side of the smoke-deflector it can be seen where both the name plate (upper) and special plaque (lower) commemorating the event had been fitted. Around this time, it became common to see locomotives without their plates, as the authorities removed them for safe-keeping. In No. 92220's case, this had apparently been done here at Tyseley in the January. No. 92220 was by this time just another grimy 2-10-0, its glory days of hauling named passenger expresses long gone, and withdrawal came two months later. No. 92220 had the shortest life of any in the 251 strong class. Indeed, it had the shortest life of any BR standard steam locomotive, although of course, it survives today in preservation. Outside the shed and looking decidedly the worse for wear on what is thought to be the same day, is Gloucester-allocated No. 7034 *Ince Castle*, which like No. 92220, has had at least one of its name plates removed. Tyseley did have 'Castles' on its own allocation until February 1965, and one of the very few express passenger workings for them latterly was the Fridays only 5.45 p.m. Birmingham (Snow Hill) to Paddington, which seems to have remained with steam until towards the end of 1964.

The rather decrepit looking station at Oxford has already been seen. Another that, but for the Second World War, would have probably been modernised a lot earlier was Banbury General, and so named from 1949 to 1969 to avoid confusion with the old LNWR station at Merton Street. It was the first major scheme of its kind undertaken on the entire Western Region of British Railways, and was finished in 1958. It is seen here in about 1960 as a northbound freight hauled by a GWR 'Mogul' passes through. The new buildings were in the style of the era, with a reinforced concrete frame structure and infilling panels of London stock bricks. The emphasis was on cleanliness, light, and fresh air. Banbury had long been a bottle-neck, with the main line having to be occupied during shunting movements, and track improvements included a new down relief line, realignment of the main lines with the speed restriction raised to 75 mph, and the lengthening and raising of the platforms.

Left, above and below: Alan had a great interest in small industrial locomotives, and in the annals of the Industrial Railway Society, he is credited with rescuing Kerr Stuart 'Wren' class narrow gauge 0-4-0 W/N 3114 in 1959. Southam Limeworks in Warwickshire purchased from Peckett and Sons of Bristol six 1-foot-11½-inch narrow gauge 0-6-0s between 1903 and 1923, and in 1934, the works, together with its locomotives, were acquired by the Rugby Portland Cement Company. All these locomotives were named following a geological theme such as *Jurassic* and *Triassic*, and the manufacturer's literature even referred to them as the 'Jurassic' class. The first photograph shows *Mesozoic*, which had a works number of 1327 and had been built in 1913. Two of them were broken up in 1943 at Southam, but *Mesozoic* was noted still at work in that year, and there seems to have been some swopping of parts between the locomotives. On 20 October 1956, the narrow gauge system at Southam was superseded by road transport, but the remaining four survived, and judging from the photographs in Alan's collection, he seems to have been directly involved in this. *Mesozoic* was acquired by dealers R. Fenwick & Co. of Brackley, and then subsequently purchased in March 1969 by G. J. Mullis of Wychbold, Worcestershire (only a few miles from Alan's house). The locomotive now resides near Bromyard, and is owned by the author's friend Bob Palmer. The second photograph shows 1936-built Hudswell Clarke 0-4-0 diesel shunter *Southam* at work on the standard gauge system. At one time after withdrawal it was on display at the nearby Great Western Pub.

We have already seen the Railway Enthusiasts' Club (REC) rail tour of 14 September 1963 at Chipping Norton. It is now just after 4.30 p.m., and the tour has arrived at Hook Norton. The through route from Banbury to Kingham had been closed in 1958 following a landslip by Hook Norton tunnel, so by this time it was operated as two separate freight only branches – Kingham to Chipping Norton, and Banbury, or more precisely Kings Sutton Junction, to Hook Norton. Iron ore traffic was of importance in this area, and because of this, a clause in the original plans stipulated that at least two long sidings and a passing loop were to be provided at every station. To the left is the cattle loading dock siding, while on the extreme right are some of the 'long sidings', in this case creating a loop line around the back of the station. The sleeper foundation in front of No. 6111 was for railing the platelayers' trolley on to the track.

The GWR 'cut off' route from Banbury to Paddington through Bicester (North from 1949) that opened in 1910 was 18 miles and 58 chains shorter than the original route via Oxford. This is Bicester (London Road from 1954 until closure in 1968) on the Buckinghamshire Railway line (LNWR from 1879) from Bletchley to Oxford that had opened in 1850. There was no connection between the two lines at Bicester, with the GWR line passing over the LNWR. However as this book is being written, Chiltern Railways are proposing a totally new through service from Oxford to London Marylebone via this station at Bicester (called Town since reopening in 1987), and a newly constructed ¼-mile double-track connection between the previously totally separate GWR and LNWR routes here, and then on through Princes Risborough and High Wycombe. The photograph is again the 1963 REC tour, and after arrival at Bicester from Oxford (Rewley Road) reversal took place before continuing to Kingham via the loop from Oxford Road Junction to Yarnton.

We are at the west end of Verney Junction on 14 September 1963 as BR '9F' No. 92112 heads towards the setting sun, the signals above the locomotive indicating it is heading towards Bicester, with the other signal controlling the Buckingham line. The main line at Verney Junction formed part of a through route between Oxford and Cambridge, and although not included in the famous 'Beeching Report' of 1963, both Verney Junction and the through route closed from 1 January 1968. Being an east-west route, it crossed many of the main lines that radiate out from London, and during the Second World War, the usefulness of this was seen as a diversionary route, with a number of junctions put in to make connections where previously they did not exist. It has been a long-held objective to restore a direct passenger service between Oxford and Cambridge, the so-called Varsity Line, and as this book is being written, steps are underway to achieve this.

Left, above and below: The rail distance from Bicester (London Road) to here at Verney Junction is only 10 miles, but the REC tour went on a very indirect route between the two. It departed Bicester at 10.48 a.m., but did not arrive at Verney Junction via Chipping Norton, Banbury, and Buckingham until 6.50 p.m., just as the sun was setting. We have already seen at Cirencester and Tetbury the efforts BR made to try and improve the economics of rural branch lines, and another example was that between Banbury and Buckingham. Two specially adapted single-unit cars were built, one station was reopened, and two new halts built of old railway sleepers, with the service introduced on 13 August 1956. By 1957, monthly carryings were up from 2,693 to 6,423. An over 400 per cent increase in traffic was later reported, plus a one-third reduction in running costs, yet the line still did not pay its way and the service was withdrawn on 2 January 1961. The stock of the 14 September 1963 REC tour is on the left in the first photograph, and being viewed by an unlikely-looking bird (!) on the platform as one of these single-unit cars arrives on a service from Bletchley to Buckingham, which survived for a further year. Verney Junction had also been a terminus for the Metropolitan Railway from London, coming in on the right, its most northerly outpost. Although closed, it was used for carriage storage, and one track was cleared to allow the REC tour to the end of the line at a level crossing just north of Winlsow Road station.

The furthest east of Alan's photographs, and one that the author was unable to identify. However, thanks to George Howe, chairman of the Great Northern Railway Society, this has now been done, and a lot of what follows is thanks to him, although much of the infrastructure visible here had disappeared before George's first memories of the site. The photograph is taken from the road bridge just north of Huntingdon Station, and looking north, it shows an 'A3' heading towards London Kings Cross with a thirteen-coach express. The big clue for George was the oil depot on the left, and now vanished, as also the down dock and crane, on the other side the up dock was still there in the early 1970's when George was a relief signalman at Huntingdon. This view is thought to date from the very early 1960s when steam haulage of the East Coast Main Line expresses to Kings Cross was coming to an end. The final scheduled workings were on Sunday 16 June 1963.

Quarrying for ironstone at Finedon, to the east of Wellingborough, was started by Rixon & Co. in 1874, and a horse tramway was laid to the Midland Railway. Ten years later, the first steam locomotive was purchased to the unusual gauge, in this country at least, of metre gauge, and 1886 saw the first furnace brought into use at Rixon's newly-built Wellingborough Ironworks. The trade depression of the late 1920s saw only a single furnace in blast, and on 22 September 1932, work ceased altogether, with the mines and quarries being closed. The Stanton Ironworks then assumed a greater measure of control, rebuilding the ironworks and increasing the efficiency of the railway; in fact, the last sustained attempt in the ironstone industry to modernise a narrow gauge system. New, long four-wheeled wagons carrying pairs of 5-ton-capacity skips on steel underframes were built with centre buckeye couplings, as seen in both photographs, and these were rotated on their trunnions to be emptied by a mobile crane specially equipped with tackle at the jib head. New locomotives were also purchased from Peckett's of Bristol in September 1934 with consecutive works numbers of 1870/71, and both are seen here carrying spark arresters. In the distance to the right of the engine shed can be seen the very narrow bore tunnel under the main line to St Pancras. The end came on 14 October 1966, and these photographs were taken on 1 October during a final visit arranged by the Industrial Railway Society.

This is the view looking north at Brixworth Station on the LNWR line from Market Harborough to Northampton. The date is 14 August 1963, and Stanier '8F' No. 48733, a Bescot allocated locomotive from 1951 until withdrawal in June 1965, is hauling a coal train towards Northampton. The line had opened in 1859, but Brixworth lost its passenger service from Monday 4 January 1960, although freight carried on, as can be seen from the photograph with a wagon in the goods yard, until 1 June 1964. In the immediate vicinity of Brixworth were no fewer than three ironstone tramways working at the same time. It also had some of the earliest and to work them with locomotives. Brixworth Old Pits, under the ownership of the Sheepbridge Co., commenced operations in 1883 using a 2-feet-gauge tramway, including cable operation with a winding drum on a double incline. The line terminated at a tipping dock in Brixworth Station goods yard, and operations ceased about 1908.

Also believed to have been photographed on 14 August 1963, these are the transhipment sidings for the Hanging Houghton and Scaldwell ironstone pits, about 1 mile north of Brixworth Station, with the Market Harborough to Northampton line on the left. Originally, both used a 3-feet-gauge system, but the demands of the Second World War required increased production that was done, not by extending the narrow gauge at Hanging Houghton, but by replacing it with standard gauge. This very steep (1 in 44), but well engineered line was built using Italian prisoner-of-war labour, under the direction of the manager of the Staveley Coal & Iron Co. Ltd. Clearly posed for photography are firstly *Robert*, built by Avonsides of Bristol W/No. 2068 of 1933, used initially at the main line sidings, as up to 1933 this had been done by gravity. The next two are *Lamport No. 2* and *Lamport No. 3*, built by Bagnalls of Stafford W/Nos 2669 & 2670 of 1942. All three were 0-6-0s.

Opposite and above: The precursor of the Industrial Railway Society was the Birmingham Locomotive Club, and it was this club that organised the visit to the Brixworth area on 14 August 1963. The Scaldwell system, as seen in these three photographs, stopped with the 3-feet narrow gauge that it had been built with in 1912 by the Lamport Ironstone Co., and it was initially connected to the LNWR main line by an elevated ropeway nearly 2 miles long. The Scaldwell quarries were much more extensive than at nearby Hanging Houghton, and were further expanded in the Second World War. Also, during the threat of invasion, the locomotives even had their names covered over with iron sheets. The entire Scaldwell system closed in December 1962, and so presumably the initial two photographs are posed. The first of which shows *Handyman,* built by Hudswell Clarke with W/N 573 in 1900 as a metre gauge locomotive. This came from Cranford Quarries in 1936 where it had been stored for the previous seventeen years. *Lamport,* an 0-6-0 built by Peckett & Sons in 1913, came as a new locomotive to Scaldwell, but by around 1961, it was in need of repairs that were started but never finished, and it is missing coupling-rods in the second photograph. *Scaldwell,* another Peckett similar to *Lamport* and consecutively numbered, was the only working locomotive by 1963, and is seen in the final photograph hauling club members along the overgrown tracks in side-tippler ironstone wagons. They were made of oak and elm, and the railway even had its own full-time carpenter who had built many of them.

An unidentified 'Peak' Type 4 diesel is heading through Market Harborough on its way to London St Pancras, probably about 1963. The Midland Division of the LMR, which was responsible for this route to Manchester and Carlisle, plus that from Derby to Bristol, took the decision late in 1957 to eliminate steam. The initial aim was to cover all long-distance main-line passenger, parcels, express freight, and mineral services. To meet this, 122 'Peak' Type 4 diesel locomotives were authorised under the 1960 Building Programme. The anticipated date for completion of this initial scheme was September 1962, and an early problem that became quickly apparent was that diesels easily coped with the steam schedules and were frequently running ahead of time. Of course, the steam power then had to be redistributed to make the most economical use of it, and this started early in 1961 when most of the 'Royal Scots' were transferred away, to be followed by the 'Jubilees' later in the year.

This is again the north end of Market Harborough Station on the same day, and amongst an array of semaphore signals are a 'WD' 2-8-0 and BR Standard Class 4 No. 75013. When considering redistribution of the remaining steam engines, there was a definite need to find suitable work for the more modern, such as No. 75013, which had only entered service in November 1951. The North Wales area had been a home to this class since first constructed, and No. 75013 had previously been at Llandudno Junction for nearly six years, their moderate axle-loading allowing them to work the circular North Wales Land Cruise trains via Corwen, Barmouth, Portmadoc, and Bangor. By 1963, No. 75013 was at Bletchley, and one month before the depot closed in July 1965, it went back to North Wales, but this time Machynlleth. Interestingly, these modest locomotives were on some days in early 1967 working 325-mile double return trips between Shrewsbury and Aberystwyth, the highest for steam anywhere in the country.

One of the last places to become a railway 'town' was the small village of Woodford Halse in a thinly populated corner of Northamptonshire. The final major rail route to London, in the pre-Channel Tunnel era, was that of the Great Central Railway, which ran from Annesley in Nottinghamshire to Quainton Road near Aylesbury, a distance of some 92 miles. By 1899, it was fully open and was designed for high-speed running with moderate gradients and curves, plus a generous loading gauge, forming a through route from Manchester, Sheffield, Nottingham, and Leicester to London. There were junctions at Woodford Halse, and so massive marshalling yards together with a major locomotive depot were established; the population soared and dedicated railway housing was built. On 9 May 1964, No. 46251 *City of Nottingham* calls at Woodford Halse hauling 'The East Midlander No. 7' rail tour from Nottingham to Didcot. Dr. Beeching's dislike of duplicate routes sealed the line's fate and it closed through Woodford Halse in September 1966.

At one time, Gresley's 'V2' class 2-6-2s were a common sight on the Great Central route, and even as late as 1959 there were three of the class allocated here at Woodford Halse. But around the time of No. 60828's visit on 9 May 1964, the nearest examples were at York depot, the shed to which No. 60828 was allocated, and it had worked in from Annesley the day previously. In 1936, the LNER freight services were accelerated when a special registered goods service was inaugurated under the name of the 'Green Arrow Service', and the 'V2' class of mixed traffic locomotives was designed to work it. In appearance, they were akin to the 'A3' Pacifics, with a similar boiler, but a 2-feet-shorter barrel. They proved exceptionally capable on the express goods services and soon found their way on to the passenger expresses. During the Second World War, their haulage abilities on the LNER earned them the reputation of the engines that won the war.

We are now at Burton-on-Trent in the early 1960s, and thanks are due to Mark Ratcliffe, chairman of the Burton Railway Society, for providing some of the information that follows. Heading towards Birmingham in the first photograph is 'WD' 2-8-0 No. 90162, which between January 1960 and withdrawal in February 1964 was allocated to Canklow shed at Rotherham. To its right can be seen the cattle dock once used for unloading animals destined for Messrs Robirch. The 'WD' stands for 'War Department', and these locomotives were a simplified version of the LMS '8F' 2-8-0, and were built during the Second World War using 20 per cent less man hours. Noticeable, was the squat little chimney, lower than the other boiler mountings. Burton-on-Trent is famous for brewing beer and this generated much traffic for the railway; the brewery companies having their own internal rail systems whose level crossings abounded in the town. The Ind Coope (the strange name deriving from Edward Ind plus Octavius and George Coope) bottling stores form the backdrop in the second photograph, as 'Crab' No. 42799 heads north past it with some stored carriages in between. This locomotive was allocated at Burton and then Nottingham between June 1959 and May 1964. Very distinctive on the 'Crabs' were the very large outside cylinders, needed because of their low boiler pressure. With the resultant high raised running plate over the cylinders and valve gear, their nickname was originally 'Land Crabs'. Also distinctive as a result of design conflicts in the early LMS, is that the tender was narrower than the engine.

Moving north, we arrive at Derby on 8 September 1957, and we find at the shed, with one the earliest of Alan's photographs in this book, Lancashire & Yorkshire Railway 'Pug' No. 51217. Fifty-seven of these tiny locomotives were built between 1891 and 1910, and No. 51217 was built at their Horwich works in 1895. The combination of a light axle-load, short-wheelbase, and excellent visibility, with the cab well above the saddle tank, enabled them to be used in sharply curved sidings virtually anywhere. The class had disc wheels and dumb (rigid) buffers instead of the usual spring-loaded variety.

BR Standard Class 4 No. 75013, in another undated photograph, is coming off the 1881-opened spur at Uttoxeter, which allowed direct running towards Stoke from the Churnet Valley line, and is displaying the lamp code for what seems to be an empty stock train. The shed code on No. 75040 appears to be that for Stoke, to where it was allocated from October 1963 until June 1967. Stoke depot became something of a refuge for the class following dieselisation elsewhere, and by October 1963, had eleven '75xxxs'. Their main use at Stoke was on local freights, but a number were stored. No. 75040 was finally withdrawn in October 1967 from Carnforth.

To bring this book to a conclusion, we return to one of Alan's favourite haunts, the Strand Lane road bridge just north of Fernhill Heath. It is autumn and the crops have been harvested as No. 7906 *Fron Hall* makes its way towards Worcester on 18 October 1964, with the fireman hosing down the coal. It was also the autumn as far as steam was concerned, although there was still a surprising amount through Fernhill Heath, particularly freight. However, within a few months *Fron Hall* will no doubt be suffering the indignity of having its name plates removed, possibly its number plates as well, before withdrawal in March 1965. By the end of 1965, all scheduled steam through Fernhill Heath will have come to an end. We owe a great debt to Alan Maund, he took the time to record the images in this book before it all vanished forever, and it has been a privilege to act as compiler of this unique and nostalgic volume.